ST. GERMAIN

TWIN SOULS
&
SOULMATES

THE I AM PRESENCE OF ST. GERMAIN
CHANNELLED THROUGH
AZENA RAMANDA AND CLAIRE HEARTSONG

TRIAD
PUBLISHERS PTY LTD

For information address:
TRIAD Publishers USA, Inc.
23623 N. Scottsdale Rd., #D-3 (146)
Scottsdale, AZ, 85255, USA
Ph: (602) 585 4287 Fax: (602) 585 2871

Book Title:

TWIN SOULS & SOULMATES

AUTHORS:

St. Germain, channelled by Azena Ramanda
St. Germain, channelled by Claire Heartsong
Book and cover design by Peter O. Erbe

COVER IMAGE:

'The Merging' - original Boddhi Batik, Sri Lanka, by courtesy of Klaus Michael Streil.

National Library Of Australia: ISBN: 0 646 21150 1

Printed in the United States of America.

*Triad Publications aim at aiding and inspiring
a spiritually unfolding humanity.*

PUBLISHER'S NOTE

The 'Twin Souls & Soulmates' material represents a compilation of teachings by the I AM Presence of St. Germain. Chapters 1-7 were channelled through Azena Ramanda during group sessions (held in the U.S.A.) within the period of 1986 to 1989.

The material contained in chapters 8 and 9 was channelled through Claire Heartsong in the U.S.A. during March, 1993.

All editing efforts were aimed at retaining St. Germain's particular style of expression, while simultaneously affording smooth reading.

Experiencing Christ-consciousness within yourself, loving unconditionally that which you are as you exist and abide in your reality at this point in time, creates the resonance within your being that attracts the identical essence within the opposite body of soul energy - your soulmate will manifest in physicality as a natural progression and merges with your energy and you with it. And as you merge together closer and closer and drink more and more of one another's cups, you become One, and you become one another's strength and one another's love. As this occurs, you experience what is called enlightenment.

- ST. GERMAIN -

When you dispense with the idea of soulmate as an entity who will bring you happiness and when you understand soulmate as the rest of humanity, then the entity - your soulmate, who will allow you the experience of happiness - will appear.

- ST. GERMAIN -

CONTENTS

CONTENTS

AN INTRODUCTION TO ST. GERMAIN

by Peter O. Erbe

To the uninitiated, the 'newcomer' to the concept of channelling, this subject may easily represent a confusing picture. Questions such as 'Why?', 'Why now?' and 'Why are so many entities being channelled?' and 'Who are they anyway?' are only too familiar. Perhaps a brief survey may offer some clarification.

Every now and then throughout human history there existed men and women who were very aware of humanity's plight of separation from its Source. These souls reached out, called for help, and as time progressed more and more souls joined the cry of the heart for liberation from separation until a point of critical mass had been reached. This created a window so to speak, enabling a two-way communication between the physical realm and higher dimensions. As human beings have free will, the call for help had to come from within humanity first and also had to carry enough weight to be sufficiently strong to create that opening.

Once this opening had been established (although individual cases of channelling have always taken place from time to time), the real season of channelling began. Beings from numerous dimensions and even other star systems began to utilize this tool now on a broad scale to help accelerate humanity's awakening as to its true identity, to coax human beings into a remembrance as to their real nature of being individualized expressions of what we call God.

As this awakening is progressing, we are approaching another point of critical mass, enabling mass-consciousness to shift from a mere third dimensional awareness to a fourth dimensional understanding. In proportion to the acceleration of man's awakening an air of excitement and joyous expectancy is forming on both 'sides'. More and more beings, humans and entities from unseen realms desire to communicate with one another, not only telepathically or

1

during dream states, but also via the direct hot-line of channelling. And it is here that this process becomes frequently diffused, if not misused through the attention seeking by not only channelling humans but by channelled entities of certain lower realms as well.

As a result pure and unfiltered channelled communications are rather infrequent. In light of this, the material presented here is priceless, as both Azena Ramanda and Claire Heartsong are pure channels. It is not uncommon for certain entities, such as St. Germain for example, to communicate through more than one channel.

The name St. Germain is a mere label to help the audience identify this entity and refers to one of his previous incarnations, also known as Count Ragoszy. There have been many other incarnations of his, some of which history recorded as Samuel, and Noah of the Old Testament, Joseph, father of Jeshua Ben Joseph, Christopher Columbus and Sir Francis Bacon. However, whenever one speaks of incarnations one ought to be mindful of the fact that any given incarnation of any soul represents only a fragment, a facet, of a much grander being. This accounts for St. Germain's preference to be addressed as 'I AM' and not as St. Germain. Although infinitely more aware of his and our true identity, he sees himself as a brother, in no way superior to earthly humans; however, to those partial to an orderly labelling of things, St. Germain refers to himself as a seventh level consciousness, compared to humanity's consciousness, which is of third and transitional fourth level. Perhaps it is best to allow St. Germain to introduce himself in his very own words, quote:

From a river born of God I come forth to reflect your divinity. Hear my call. We of the Council of Light have come so that you may know our joy as One. I come because you have called the essence of the Brotherhood of the Light unto you. I come as an equal brother, divine being of light that recognizes your divine beingness of light. I come to share with you. I come because I love you! I love you beyond your imaginings. I wish not to be revered or captured within any image that will be placed upon your wall. That I do not desire. I desire to free you unto your own vision of God and, indeed, you are becoming One with GOD I AM.

Chapter 1

THE MEANING OF RELATIONSHIPS

We [channelled entities] are all here upon this plane to reflect unto you that which you are for the purpose of guiding you back unto yourselves, after eons of division and separation between yourself and the divine creative essence - the Father/Mother within, the Source. Indeed, we are here in joy to express and assimilate the light upon this plane, to allow the divine creative force to flow through you in harmonic balance. Truly beauteous you all are and you do not know this yet. You are on the verge of coming consciously into the awareness of this. You all have this knowingness inwardly, on a soul essence level, of the grand divine force that you all are, but you are not aware of it as such in physicality. Indeed, what you are is beyond physicality. Some upon this plane have termed it 'metaphysical', for that is indicative of being beyond the physical, but there is more even than what is termed 'metaphysical'.

You are indeed the creative force that is known as God, which is omniscient, omnipresent and all powerful - omnipotent. As God, you all are all powerful - the force flows through you and exemplifies itself through your embodiment. What you create as outer life circumstance is also your creative expression as God.

Your relationship - what is it but a reflection of you? It is the creative force within another essence that you call your lover, your mate, your husband, your sibling, your family. All of it in totality is that reflection of you in its myriad frequencies. It is of *One* essence and that essence is God. That essence is the creative force that you express before you in the mirror of reflective experience so that you may garner from it the wisdom of what is you.

Why is it that love is so wondrous and mysterious to all of you that you search your lives for eon after eon to find the perfect love? Why indeed? It is because it is a reflection of you that you can see in physicality, which you can know and understand in physicality. Indeed, it is what *you* are and for which you are searching so fervently. That which is you is exemplified and understood and felt as the emotion of love, for that is God. God is love. God is love in its myriad of forms. The God, the relationship and the love, for which you so fervently search, is *you*.

You, my dearest brothers and sisters, are in limitation upon this plane and that is why you perceive joy as being outward of you and not inward of you. Therefore, there is separation and what you express as a relationship is separate of you. You do not understand relationships as unity with the Source, but as a co-mingling with something outside yourself.

What indeed is a relationship? It is connection. It is belonging. What is belonging? It is union, unified harmony with the God source within the restraints of physicality, within the limitation that you understand as dense physical matter on this plane. In super-consciousness it will not remain long in the limitation that you perceive now at this point in time.

However, the transition between third and fourth density, your unfoldment into the God-essence, allows you to have all your circumstance and all your relationships mirrored unto you as love exemplified.

What is the relationship with a family, a sibling, with the heart of your being? Indeed, it is the reflection from the beginning. Eon after eon you have experienced what it is to be mother or father, to have unequaled love for family. You have experienced the harbouring of bitterness, of resentment and the purging of all the relationships that you would consider to be disharmonious and to be uncomfortable. All of this is for you to understand that which you are.

Whatever discomforts you is the discomfort and misalignment with the divine element within you known as Alter Ego. Indeed, this is a divine part of you. All that is part of you is divine and this is merely one element of you. Alter Ego may express itself in clinging to what is physical in nature, to the misalignment known as pain, to the misunderstanding of other entities, to the creation of war on this plane and clinging to all sorts of ailments in its myriad forms.

Disharmony, or misalignment, merely serves as a mirror for you so you may see what it is that is you. You think you are in love with others, indeed. *You are not.* You are in love with what others mirror unto you that is *you*. You understand this as separation. Within super-consciousness you will understand this as union, as merging and as the undefinable balance between what you consider to be your separate Self and your SELF. There will be no separation known in super-consciousness.

With an all-consuming, burning desire you seek to have harmony with your love, the entity who is the object of your affection. 'What may I do to cure the argumentative nature of this other entity', this warring between the two of us - what will I do to cure the disharmony?' In all myriads and fashion of forefronts which present themselves upon your experience, you wish to mend the division. Unification is the healer and is divine harmony exemplified. Disharmony is only the perception of your misalignment, for indeed, in the unlimited version of it all, there is really no disharmony. The Source which is unconditional love, which is the Isness of the divine Father/Mother, is allowing of it all without judgment. It is you who judge whether one particular circumstance is better than another.

It is judgment to see one relationship as better than another, whether it be a relationship with a lover, with an employer or with any of the entities you have contact with in your daily activity. They are all divine in their own understanding and generate their wisdom for you to capture and garner within you that which is *you* within the circumstances. You see, what you judge in another entity, is *you*. You cannot identify anything within any circumstance or entity that you have not been before, for the resonance of identification is the resonance of it and part of yourself together in harmony. That is called recognition.

Now, as we continue with this, we intend to unveil a knowingness within you of the relationship you have with your being, a relationship that is joyous, allowing the effervescence of life in happiness. Happiness is within *you*. It is not within the relationship. It is not out here, not out there. Nothing is out here. What you gaze unto as the relationship, whether it is joyous or whether it is disharmonious - that is only a mirror, *it is your judgment of yourself* as exemplified in this mirror of a relationship. The meaning of a relationship is merely the recognition of you in circumstance. If you understood who you are, you would always have harmony within any relationship, whether it be an employment situation, your family unit, your lover, or with a mere stranger. They are all relationships and they all are initial understandings of your relationship with humanity - with life.

Humanity itself is the spectrumized version of every entity. All of you in humanity are multi-dimensional aspects of God as human life existence upon this plane. Also exemplifications of God and life experience are your flora and fauna, your plants and animals which are loving, nurturing and very healing essences. The disharmony they experience within their circumstances is merely the reflection they garner for their own gaining of wisdom, for they also unfold. It is not the same dimension and expansion as that of humanity, but they also unfold. As the reflections of all the spectrumized versions of life are exemplified and mirrored to one another and are gaining access to their light, the grand unlimited essence of them, which is of God, is coming into union, into the knowing of the merging of the divine creative force. When this occurs there will be peace, harmony and joy upon this plane in all relationships. Indeed, it will be understood as super-consciousness or the age of Aquarius and all the other terminologies it is known as. Indeed, this will be the coming of age of relationships without limitation, for all will be in relation to another, ad infinitum as it were. All will be in the understanding of the relationship between themselves as reflections of one another, facets of themselves experienced as other entities.

The union and the merging of this entire Earth plane, whether it be of inanimate, animate or non-physical essence, whatever it is, as it merges into the energy form that is known as God, will come into the understanding of ascension. This will be the merging of the light - of the bodies of energy which are frequency bundles called personalities or essences in and of themselves. It will reflect the dichotomized understanding of separation through unity. This is God.

There is indeed that God, the grand creative force, that is All-That-Is, which contemplated itself to create all of this, but *you* are that God. This is the dichotomy. As you come into the knowing of your divine nature, the Christ within you is mirrored to all who are existent upon this plane, is reflected and reflected and reflected in an infinite understanding. Then being lovers will be experienced with joy in the heart and it will not be superficial in any form or fashion. God will be exemplified and the other gender will be experienced as the mate of your being, as soulmate. Does this sound familiar to any of you?

There has been much 'hoop-la' about this particular word 'soulmate'. You indeed have a soulmate upon this plane. Indeed, there is the other essence of you which is physical and non-physical; gender of yourself and of the opposite gender. So, the fervent search, the burning desire to know God exemplified as the other gender, will come to fruition in super-consciousness and the relationship with a lover will be none other than the relationship with the other facet of you. The body of your essence will be identical. *Indeed, it will be the resonance within your being with yourself in another fashion or form that is physical.* There will be more than one [soulmate] as well. In the measure of your understanding of this, what is superficial in nature will dissipate. There will be no further use for this, for the understanding of the Alter Ego exemplifying itself within the relationship in lust, hatred, jealousy, resentment, bitterness and pain - all of these understandings will, as you call it, go 'poof'. Does this sound like a thing you would be interested in? Indeed, so be it.

The unified harmony within super-consciousness, within the light of this Earth plane, resonating through this dimension unto a myriad of other dimensional experiences and infinitely resonating back unto you - much likened unto a ricochet effect - will come into the knowingness of each of you. The relationship you have with your lover, with a mate, will be of harmony, for it will be in the understanding of your divinity. It will be outwardly known as Christ-consciousness exemplified.

Christ-consciousness may be experienced now in totality upon your Earth plane. Indeed it may be. It need not abide until super-consciousness, as you sit and tap your foot. *It is not necessary to wait. You may have joy, which is experienced as utter ecstasy,* but there is a necessity, because of the limitation upon your plane, for the *allowance of another's divinity.* That is unconditional love exemplified unto them. How else will you come into the understanding of unconditional love of yourself, but through this mirror of you? Indeed, this is a harmonious relationship, free of pain, of disharmony, and this merely through allowing the other entity's sovereignty. This is understood as humility, the allowance of your own sovereignty to unfold unto yourself, to allow the balancing of yourself to occur and to allow them the same in their own ripeness.

Unconditional love will be felt throughout your planet. It is already occurring in governments and political structures, in the races, creeds, religions and even the genders that have been warring throughout eons in your time. It is coming into alignment. It is coming into the harvest of knowingness. Indeed, it shall be grand upon your land when the light is exemplified in all through unconditional love and through this unconditional love you will allow them their sovereignty, allow them their bitterness, their jealousies, their resentment - for this is their Alter Ego mirrored unto them and it is alright. There is no judgment at all. In God-awareness and God-knowingness of SELF, that which you consider to be yourself is nothing but SELF. The barrier, the definition of separation in and of itself, will dissolve. When this dissolution occurs, you will find yourself extending beyond your own auric field, beyond your light body, beyond the auric field of your planet into what you now call cosmic awareness! It is merely the awareness of the unity of all life through you. That is all it is. There is nothing mystical about it and nothing to be feared. There is nothing unusual, for it is very usual to have the knowingness of unity of all other life when you are within the knowingness of your divinity and of your sovereignty.

As you reign supreme and walk in sovereignty and in dominion of your creation, indeed, there is nothing to fear. As you become co-creators and manifestors, you will quite naturally, as a progressive understanding of this, manifest harmonious circumstances within a relationship. It is only natural.

I will allow open forum for a moment.

Questions And Answers.

Q: I have a question regarding my understanding of denial and allowance. I would rather experience joy, so I would put my attention on that rather than feel the pain which can become so repressed that I am not even aware that it is there. But that truly is denial, it is not unconditional love. So, I can understand intellectually to allow, but I do not know how to embrace that emotionally, to truly love it.

Oh, but you do know how. You are merely not feeling it with your heart. All entities have all knowing within their soul essence and that is grander than their expression known as physicality. All have equally as much knowing as I do. All are in divine equality. The denial of part of SELF is the severance of it, the separation of it, and it will accomplish disharmony. There is nothing wrong with the disharmony, for there is much to be garnered within that situation. Indeed, there is much wisdom to be had. However, if you would desire to have the fruits of harmony within your experience, within relationships and with SELF, you would have to allow the knowingness of the sovereignty of SELF, the knowingness of the divine nature in every heartbeat and in every pulsation, that YOU ARE GOD. Your embodiment is mystery amplified in physicality, but so are you. It [the physical embodiment] is the result of you. As you have awe, respect and love for yourself, you will not have the urge to deny any part of it, even that part of it that gives you a bit of discomfort from time to time - that which you consider to be Alter Ego. As you come into this understanding, discomfort will dissipate, for discomfort is of third density understanding. It is Alter Ego immersed in physicality, clinging to the Earth plane. As you release it into the All-That-Is and give it up into the Source, into the wisdom of the knowingness you have already captured, you will ignite the torch of freedom within your heart. The spark of life within you will create joy and the joy within will not allow you to contemplate yourself as anything else than what you would desire to be. Therefore there will be no need to desire or choose anything that would deny part of you. The denial of your - as you call it - mental process will give you friction, frustration and the severance of a part of you. It will give you some amount of pain and that will not be in super-consciousness. Pain will not be apparent in super-consciousness. The pain you feel when your heart is broken in a relationship is exactly the pain you would feel if your heart were physically broken. Indeed, it is broken. It is weeping blood. It is a painful tearing - the ripping and rending of your soul essence.

Indeed, catch the wisdom from it, let it seep into and nourish and nurture the divine essence of you - the grander essence of you which you do not perceive with your blinkers on. When you release these blinkers, you will experience joy rather than disharmony. You will cry and weep with joy, not with sorrow. The salty nectar, the juice of the soul, waters the land upon which you stand and you will also nourish life about you and you will flourish in all that you are, in your beingness. You will BE divine. Your tears will be filled with the essence of God and they will infiltrate the auric field of all they encounter and give unto them the understanding of God. So tears are wondrous indeed. They allow God to come forward and experience emotion. You also cry when you are angry and when you are frustrated, and you also cry when you have fear. Every emotion is merely one other frequency of the spectrum of Isness. It is all divine. There is nothing wrong with pain. There is nothing wrong with sorrow. There is nothing wrong with disharmony with a mate or a relationship. It is a frequency to be harmonized and resonated to within your being so you may understand all the spectrum within - the Isness of you. Doing this, you find no need to continue resonating to it, for it is already resonating, so you may move on into the understanding of the totality of the spectrum.

Joy is merely a higher octave of pain. It is an enlightened version of pain. Disharmony and discord within any relationship will release itself in the joy of the Isness of the circumstances. When you walk into a whirlwind circumstance or confront an entity who you do not desire outwardly to be present, you may place yourself before them in the understanding of your sovereignty:

I am God exemplified in physicality and I understand this circumstance as the reflection of myself in Thee. I am that I am as presented in the Isness of I. I will bring forth joy and divine harmony within any circumstance and I will allow that to encompass my being.

The reflection is all about you. It is everywhere. Colour, for example - how you respond to colour is also reflecting you. What is tonal in nature - your music - it is symphonic in the reflection of you. This reflection does not only concern the relationship with another entity, but the relationship with every single frequency you encounter; whether it be in the form of art or in what you adorn yourself with; or whether it be in nature and how you respond to it. Your resonance to certain locales on this Earth, or how you have relationships with different continents, is reflective of you.

The creative force resonates to what you so desire and manifests the circumstances about you. You may walk with the desire for Christ-consciousness to come forward in every single relationship and so mirror unto them what they are. Thus they come more and more into their own light and each entity will unfold unto themselves. They will come to know the God they are and super-consciousness will prevail upon your plane and you will experience more and more freedom. You will perceive without judgment. Therefore, in the awareness of All-That-Is, all the entities you come into contact with in your daily life, will reflect you and you gather more and more knowingness about SELF. What is a relationship but an experience with SELF?

I love you all so grandly. I desire so fervently for all of you to know your brilliance. You are so wondrous. You are galaxies. You are splendid in your nature. You are exemplifying the All-That-Is in a form that is beauteous, that is creative, that is art in and of itself. Art is not outside of you, it *is* you. Express it *as you*, as the Isness of you, that is being creative. Paint love upon the canvas of relationships. Paint upon it peace. Paint upon it beauty. Beauty is not physical, but beauty is creating the physical. All of you are coming into the awareness of this, bit by bit. Life is beauty. Life is love. Life is God - the Trinity. God exemplified in man will illuminate all the other parts of BEING with the light of its own Isness. The IS is God. The God that you understand to be the grand creative force is merely the understanding of all of you in the totality of life in relationship with one another in your myriad of forms, whether it be conflicting or not. War is indeed the Isness as well. War - the reflection of you that is Alter Ego - is divine, for all is divine - there is no thing that is not. For all, whether it be a circumstance, a situation, an entity, or even a life form that is inanimate, was created of God - of the Source. Is there a question?

Q: You said that if one is with someone, that there is a reflection of one's Alter Ego - did I hear that right?

If the relationship is disharmonious.

Q: Oh. But it can also be a reflection of light?

The totality of you, including your Alter Ego, is light. The Divine Ego of SELF is also presented in the reflection of another entity. That which is of judgment is what is separating you and that is what tells the difference.

Q: How can I change that?

As I spoke before, come into a circumstance with the acknowledgment that either part of you, whether it be Alter Ego or Divine Ego, is indeed divine, is indeed God and is part of you. Acknowledge it, embrace it and love it, for it is you. As you do this, you become less and less judgmental of yourself and circumstances.

Q: St. Germain, could you speak of the mutual devotion between a man and a woman without giving one's power away in such a relationship?

I shall. Love of one another in the mutual understanding that one is desirous to offer *all* of SELF unto this entity explodes into divine harmonic union. This will result in harmony without giving your power away, because you are in the understanding of one another's sovereignty. It is not bowing before another entity. It is bowing of each unto the other, for each respects the God within the other. In this manner the source of compassion and unconditional love of SELF is reflected by this other entity. So, as you have unconditional love of SELF, sovereignty is presented before you as sovereign circumstance.

The two together in union and harmony, will express honour of each other's sovereignty. This will occur regardless of what the other entity would expect of himself, because this light of you is reflected back unto you ad infinitum. Being in your auric field, it is quite natural that this other entity will consume the same knowingness, the awareness that is yours. This entity will reflect you and identify within at soul level. The blossoming and unfoldment of this other entity is quite natural. You call it following along, but this understanding is sequential in nature and that is limited.

Now, understanding an intimate relationship with another entity as the relationship between yourself and God, you will come to understand also the relationship between you and your own gender. Super-consciousness is not male, nor is it female - it is both. It is equal, unisexual in nature, or androgynous. It is an expression of the alignment and the harmony, the *balance* of the two genders. You see, for eons of time females have been in submission and have been giving their power away, believing their sovereignty is a no-thing. The male on your Earth believed for eons his sovereignty was the only one that counted. This belief system created the slave-drivers, the lack of unconditional love, the judgment. Why is it so many of your judges have been male? You are now coming into the alignment of both in equality. This has begun a decade ago in your time and it is gaining momentum. It will continue to gain, until the harmony between the genders - that grand explosion of knowingness - occurs.

It will take place as a birthing of a new understanding of womankind and that womankind will be sovereign indeed. It will take the male quite by surprise. It will reign as equal. It will govern SELF as equal. It will permit unconditional love to flow and submission or humility to merge with sovereignty so that there is a harmonious union within the female in and of itself. So also will the male come into alignment with the Source, with the sovereignty of All-That-Is, in balance with humility. It will indeed express more mellowness, as you would call it. Sovereignty is merely the knowingness that *I am sovereign. I am unified harmony in dominion over my kingdom. I am that I AM.* This is sovereignty.

Unified maleness and femaleness will not harbour within it fear of the other gender, for the fear of the other gender is merely the Alter Ego being in fear of the mirror the other gender presents - the fear of your own sovereignty as expressed by the males, and the fear of your own submission or humility as expressed by the females. This fear will dissipate.

The preference for your own gender - you understand of which I speak - this will dissipate also when the mellowing occurs, for the preference for the same gender is merely the fear of the other gender. It is fear at soul essence level. There is terror within of allowing one's SELF to be completed, to have the other half of SELF become unified.

As this preference dissipates, so also will the grand diseasement upon your plane. That is one of the reasons it is here, to allow the genders to merge in lack of fear of one another. This grand diseasement is indeed an *aid*, an aid to the unfoldment, to the enrichment of the Source. It is not to be feared. Fearing it will invoke a resonance in what you fear and bring it forward, likened unto a tuning fork. So do not fear this grand diseasement. Respect it and allow it to be in the sovereignty of its Isness and you will be aligning yourself to the Source within you.

As you sparkle in the kingdom of foreverness, and as the crystal of you becomes apparent in your own knowingness and therefore in the knowingness of all others, you illuminate yourself. Through that, you illuminate and enlighten all who are about you and you will find relationships take on a different hue, a different colour, a different nature. It will blend into pastel, for it will be immersed in light. It will not be so heavy and dense. Relationships will abide with you as a knowingness of kinship with God, of kinship with the fragments of God in prismatic forms which are presented as other entities, which are presented as relationships.

There is also another dichotomy. You will be both clear and unclear. Adjectives will cease to exist and the only noun that will be, is JOY. Adjectives are judgments. Clear is judgment and unclear is judgment, for there is separation between the two. When you find yourself defining over and over again, you will find yourself separating over and over again. Even the word 'Christ' is a definition. Christ and that which is not Christ is all divine. All of life, regardless of how it is exemplified, is created of a divine thought which is God. Whether you are 'Christians' or not, it is all divine and in harmony with All-That-Is. Free yourself of your judgmental nature and surrender to the Source of you and you will have harmony within SELF.

Take a day of your time, any day, it does not matter, and partake of it with absolute awareness of yourself. Go through this day and count how many judgments you make, how many separations you create and how many definitions or delineations are part of your day. How often do you partake of what you call right or wrong, good or bad, better or best - aligning yourself to the non-acceptance of the divine nature of all? However, when you align yourself to the divine nature of All-That-Is, whatever dire circumstance or heinous act of crime it may be, you will know that all is in the Isness for the creative process of learning. *Physicality is learning.* A relationship with another entity is merely partaking of a circumstance so that you can learn about yourself and see yourself in a mirror. That applies to any circumstances in your Earth plane experience, regardless of how they present themselves. If they would present themselves as what you call the loss of life - it is merely the experience of the transition of an entity, or many entities, and this is alright. It is the experience of the mutual consent of all these entities for the grander understanding, to partake of the grander wisdom within this set of circumstances.

In this understanding there is no victim, no pity, no heartbreak and no dire poverty. When you come into Christ-consciousness, the understanding that what you are is God, then there will be no pain. In all these circumstances, it is apparent that divine thought is creating the outward experience for leaping into the core of it and capturing a bouquet of wisdom. Indeed, it is created for a divine purpose.

This Earth plane is rampant with dire circumstance and it will indeed continue for a while to allow those the experience, who would desire to partake of it. Those entities who are coming into their own, cease their judgment of it.

When you understand circumstance in this light, the non-physical energy of you - of your other dimensional SELF - will be electro-magnetically attracted and will attach and merge itself into that Isness of you that is upon this Earth plane. In this manner it will experience this Earth plane in non-physical form. This is called enlightenment. It is a gathering of your energy unto you. It is called Christ-consciousness. There is nothing mystical or puzzling about it at all. There is nothing dogmatic in this understanding, for the dogma that has been attached to Christ-consciousness for eons of time is limitation. It is ritualistic for the comfort and the ease of relations within this Earth plane for a time. It indeed was purposeful. There is grand divine purpose within every circumstance. Christ-consciousness within you is unfolding into knowingness. It is becoming an awareness of the relationships you have with other entities.

You see, another entity may be of argumentative nature and Christ-consciousness within you will enable you to see yourself as argumentative. You will come into the situation with humility and love of this other entity as part of yourself and the bickering will cease.

Now, dire circumstance in an intimate relationship, jealousy for example, is merely a fear. It is the lack of understanding of your own sovereignty. That is all it is. If you knew you were God, and that you have created the circumstance, then you would have no reason to have the fear in your heart that is called jealousy, for you will be sovereign unto yourself as God. You will know your worth - your value - and you have no need to prove it to another. This 'proof of your pudding' as you call it, is merely the fervent desire to prove unto yourself who you are, not to prove to anyone else. It may appear that way, but it is not. The heart and core of it is that you are here to experience *you*. Life is for *you* to romp within, and as you play in the playground of this Earth plane, you will come into maturity, into the wisdom of your instruments of play called relationships. Indeed.

Q: St. Germain, greetings. What is it about loneliness in a person that causes them to grasp outwardly for their God SELF?

It is the desire for love that is unconditional, that is non-judgmental, for that which will love you regardless of whether you have those funny things in your hair or whether you have the apparel or the perfection of facial features that is not particularly perfect in another's eyes. Indeed, this is what you desire so fervently - unjudgmental love of you. *It is only coming unto you when you have unjudgmental love for yourself,* for what will be reflected by another entity unto you, is only the recognition of that which you already have within you. So, as you search and you peek around every corner and have minor coronary when someone sits beside you, indeed, this will continue as the search goes on.

When you are a lonely, deserted entity, longing and yearning for love, it will not come unto you, my dearest, unless you have unconditional love for yourself. When you understand the flowering of the beauty of *you*, when you gaze into the mirror and see the jewel of *you*, the pearl of *you*, the multifaceted gemstone that you are, then the light within is reflected and exhibited as colour and hue without, for you are myriad in spectrum, in beauty and in light, if only you could see it. If you could see your illumination - the golden aura of you

- you would indeed find the truth of this verbiage. What you see as yourself is not all of you. Your embodiment is merely a small fragment, is merely a facet of you. You are ultimately infinite. It is not seen by the eye or felt by the sensation of your touch, but it is you in unidentifiable form. It is omnipotent, omniscient, omnipresent and cannot be defined in any particular manner. You are the glory of God exemplified on this Earth plane. Indeed, gaze into the mirror and see this ball of light that is you, and not the physical feature! You do not see this, for you only identify with that small fragment of you. See light. See God and, as you do this, you will come to love yourself. You will cease that fervent search to end your loneliness. You will come into the knowingness of *you* and as a result of this, *you will have another entity reflected unto you who you would call soulmate.* The experience of that relationship will reflect your knowingness of your own divinity. Indeed, what is known as loneliness is a sickness of the soul. It is an ailment, a misalignment to God. It is felt as pain. It is felt as an emptiness, as a void. The void is merely a lack of knowing, a non-acknowledgment of part of SELF. That is why there is an emptiness, because it seems as if part of yourself is missing. It is not missing. It is not acknowledged.

Q: St. Germain, greetings. Whenever someone judges me, instead of just accepting it, I find I want to reach out and make a judgment back and then I somehow feel better. How can I deal with that?

On this Earth, that has been called revenge of a sort. In times past it has been considered sweet. Now it is considered Isness. There is no judgment whether revenge is good or bad. It simply is. That part of yourself that desires to do thus must be allowed to do thus. Do not contemplate yourself as bad or as being less than God when you acknowledge that there is judgment within you, for this is acknowledgment of your Alter Ego that is expressing itself. Align it to the light of you. Align it to God within you. Consider this that you would judge, that you would wreak revenge upon, as mirror. Would you do this to yourself? Would you do this to an expression of you in another form? Consider and contemplate this when you find yourself in a choice situation as this. You will find that at times you will do as you have done and this is alright, there is no judgment here. This is what you call transition and there will be a bit of both cohabitating together within you. However, as you become more enlightened, into more unified harmony with the light, you will be doing less of what the Alter Ego desires, for it will align with the desires of the Divine Ego of SELF. There will be no separation. So do not judge yourself harshly for judging, when it comes forward from time to time. Merely allow it to be and love it and as it is expressed in this manner, it will dissipate.

However, when you do find yourself in circumstances such as this, merely say to yourself: 'Aha, this is an opportunity for me to garner more light for myself. Shall I indeed wreak vengeance upon another part of myself?' For you see, it is a mirror. It is not another entity really. It may appear to be so, but it is *you*, in the brotherhood of man, that is all a unified whole. It is all ONE. You see, being in the light is also transitory in nature. As you are in the light, you are separate from the light and not one with the light. So be ONE with the light. *Be* the light, not in the light. You understand?

Q: St. Germain. Could you address the people who are not in an intimate relationship and yet feel totally complete?

The feeling of completeness, of harmony without the necessity of an outward reflection of this particular union of SELF is merely the acknowledgment of the Divine Ego of SELF and the union it already has experienced with its Alter Ego, where male and female has come into harmony and alignment within. So there is no yearning for an intimate relationship, no need for it to be expressed outwardly, for it is already in the Isness and in the knowingness of you. That is why there are so many of you who have no particular desire for a thing or a relationship, because before, in your Isness, you have experienced this and you have garnered the wisdom and nurtured yourself with it. Therefore you have no further urge to experience this particular circumstance. It is experienced as the totality of SELF. It is *you*. Is this helpful?

Q: Yes. The other question is that sometimes there is a hole within me because I have not experienced family, but at the same time I feel perfectly good..

This is judgment of yourself, indeed, for mass consciousness, social consciousness, plays harshly on you. As you partake of mass consciousness, the awareness outside of yourself, you will at times feel pressure. You judge yourself and other entities judge you to do this, or that, to have this or that experience. However, as you come into the realignment and realization of the sovereignty of you and the desire of your heart from your own soul essence, you will know what is ripe for you - not right, but ripe. When you feed on social consciousness or mass consciousness, putting yourself into a steampot as you would call it, you may release the pressure of society by feeling love for yourself: The love of you in the circumstances that you have exemplified as your heart's desire and loving the other entities who have given you an opportunity to gaze upon another facet of yourself. You see, what will diminish judgment is to contemplate and appreciate every response you have as a result of a reflection through another entity. It is an opportunity to know yourself through a relationship, regardless of how it exhibits itself, regardless of whether you would judge it to be good or bad. It is wondrous indeed, for within every single cell of your being, there is the desire for further nurturing of the light. As you feed and nourish yourself, and come into the knowing of yourself through all the other entities upon your plane, the cells of your body which are physical in nature dissipate. They will no longer be physical cells, that is dense, coarse, in the understanding of physical dense matter. They will be light. It will be energy exemplified in less dense form and as you come into an even greater understanding, your energy becomes amorphous, no form at all, not even light. Light is only a denser version of energy.

Reflect upon one another, upon your divinity, and you will understand the sameness between all of you - the union of all of you. Therefore there will be no division, separation or judgment. As you become aware of this union, there will not even be any separation of the genders, for you will all be homogenous - God exemplified in form, acknowledging one another as other facets of the Source, as other facets of SELF, as facets of the divine prism of God.

Light: All of you have it, all of you are one grand ball of light, but you are all resonating to different vibrations. All of you have within you different bundles of energy known as frequencies which give you what you call personality. That is what personalities are: different frequency bundles in consciousness, expressing as personalities. As you expand into the entire spectrum, you will not have a particular frequency resonating as a personality, for you will all have the knowing of the entire spectrum. You will not subscribe to a particular sign of the astrology chart, for you will expand into them all as you increase in your unlimitedness.

Q: You said that ultimately there would really be no soulmates - we would all be soulmates so to speak?

You will join with the energy that is likened unto you, originally separated from the Source and known as the original thirteen. Indeed, this is your mate of soul, both male and female, but in your knowingness, in the heart of your being, you will recognize and acknowledge the nature of all humanity as a brotherhood. In the ascension process, the merging with the Source, there is no separation at all. Indeed, then you will be One, and there is no soulmate at that point, *for you have merged with it.*

I will bid you all farewell for now. Partake of yourselves with joy. Share in the love which you all are. Partake of each other's auric field with reverence and awe of what is reflected back unto you, as you. I indeed partake of such gatherings with this understanding, the understanding of joy, fellowship and communion with my brothers who are equal unto that which be I.

As you would desire further communion with that which be I, bring forth merely the divine thought and it will resonate unto the essence called I and that will come forward unto you and hold your hand, as it were. So be it indeed. I leave you now with one thought. Allow it to cogitate. Let it simmer, and this thought is JOY. Bring forward this joy, this laughter, this hearty ecstasy, reverence and relishment for this plane. Partake of even uncomfortable circumstances with joy. Sing unto yourselves. Become the symphony that you have always desired to have around you. Sing unto all of life as reflections of you. Let your heart pulsate with love. As I go hence now and merge with the Source, the divine Father/Mother within, I acknowledge and embellish you. I have enjoyed immensely being in your audience, for I have partaken heartily of your light and I do express gratitude and appreciation for the brilliance of you. So be it. I shall bid you all farewell for now.

Namaste.

Chapter 2

SOULMATES

It is my honour to be in your presence and I greet you in humility and love unbounded.

Soulmates - does that bring forth a spark within your heart, a glow upon your countenance? Some of you go into the marketplace, gazing across the shoulder and become quite fluttered for fear of missing them if they should walk by. Some of you already know that your soulmate abides upon the plane. Those already understand the essence that be the other part of their soul. Understanding this is no more than understanding that which be you. You know this? There is much to be said here in your time about soulmates, but really a soulmate is Godmate. To come forth into God you must understand what it is that is coming forth into God, that which be you. It is to blossom into the blush of love. Indeed, you will become enraptured with the love of SELF. To fall in love with your SELF, to become indeed enamoured with that grand God reflected unto you in your mirror called soulmate.

Now, how do you do this? First of all, would you desire to come into countenance with that which be *you, the exact you that you are right now this very moment of your time, not the you that you are as a realized God?* Many of you would judge this other entity: 'Oh, but he's only three foot tall and green,' but beauty is beyond the skin. The Christ, the jewel of God is the essence, the etheric body, and that cannot be captured through an image. That cannot be captured in a description of physicality, for it is infinite. Do you see? So if you would desire to come into countenance with your soulmate, you must understand what it is you are desirous of coming into countenance with.

Now, in describing that enigmatic essence that you have called soulmate, I will begin at the beginning where there really is no beginning. It is called creation. Indeed, when the divine creative force, the God I Am, the Mother/Father principle - the essence of All-That-Is - contemplated itself, it expanded and separated itself. In this division it understood separation and density known as light. The electrum came forth into a lower frequency, therefore a body of light, of God essence energy, was born. At this point the male/female principle arose. For indeed within the light there are positive and negative charges, and the understanding of the separation between the two of them is the understanding of your male soulmate essence and your female soulmate essence. The entire energy body of creation was divided into maleness and femaleness. Within the male body of energy, there exist multitudinous frequencies or bundles of soul essences, complete within themselves. This is likewise also for the female body of energy. Therefore, this creates multitudinous male soulmates and multitudinous female soulmates within the same soul body energy essence.

There were thirteen of these energy bodies created. Within your male soulmate energy essence, there abides a certain frequency that is indeed identical to the same frequency in the female soulmate energy essence. Even though there are all these multitudinous soul essences within the soul body which are of different frequencies and which are indeed whole unto themselves, *there are identical frequencies existing in the opposite bodies of energy, and these you call twin flames.* This is what most think of when they consider their soulmate, but indeed, even the twin flames are not contained within one physical embodiment. There is too much energy for it to be contained within one physical embodiment. So it is physicality and non-physicality together. This is the way it is with all soulmates. You have female soulmates, plural, and you have male soulmates, plural. This plurality is at times considered as one soulmate. So there is no contradiction in this explanation, it is merely an expanded explanation.

Now, *experiencing Christ-consciousness within yourself, loving unconditionally that which you are as you exist and abide in your reality at this point in time, creates the resonance within your being that attracts the identical essence within the opposite body of soul energy. It calls it forth and merges with your energy and you with it. As this occurs, you experience what is called enlightenment.* You come more into the light because the light energy of you is coming unto you. You also become lighter in density, in weight, in illumination, in knowingness, and in joyousness.

Your soulmate affects you and you affect it constantly, and I speak of it as a body of energy which contains all the essences of soulmates. Whenever you capture the emotion of an experience, that experience is also understood by your soulmate. When a caged bird calls out in joy to a gilded bird that soars in freedom across the morning sky, the free bird responds in recognition. They respond unto one another with joy in their breasts, for indeed, animals have soulmates too. You do this as well. When you experience joy, or sorrow, or fervent anger, your soulmate feels a headache, or a questionable ache of the belly. 'What did I eat? Where did that come from?' Indigestion of your soulmate, and it need not be a physical indigestion, but an indigestion of soul essence - uncomfortable to partake of.

What you understand as deja vu at times - not all the time, but at times - is your soulmate experiencing that, so you also experience that in a manner. What you understand at times as precognition is you experiencing your soulmate's energy. All that you understand as psychic phenomena is understood by your soulmate. Now, when separation ceases between the two, that is when your joy comes. When you are in dire search, desperately seeking love, just beyond your grasp, just around the corner - 'Where oh where be my soulmate? Soulmate, soulmate, where art thou?' - when you search for this essence, in physicality or not, you will never find it, for the search will lead you right back to your own soul. The journey is a journey of knowingness of the joy of the SELF in the moment, and when you appreciate, acclaim and indeed acknowledge your life experience of the now, you will reflect it outwardly. *It will manifest accordingly.*

When you give forth love to the Earth plane in expedient fashion, having forgiveness, unconditional love, and without judgment in your heart, then it is automatically reflected back unto you - *automatically.* That is how the universe that you create for yourself responds to your divine thought energy. It allows you to create what you issue forth. As you issue forth love, love is brought back unto you for you to experience as your manifested creation.

So, this also applies to judgment. You are hard pressed at times not to judge, are you not? For what be judgment and what be observation, and what be preference, oh what a perplexity!? And this is alright, for indeed, they are merely subtle differences and the difference is the intention of the heart. Preference is your own divine heart's essence desire, but giving validity to the non-preference. When validity is not given unto non-preference, then it becomes judgment.

Now, many of you scurry for enlightenment. 'Oh what be the path that is quickest?' This is alright, but I will tell you this: There is no shortcut to soulmates, to enlightenment, to God realized. There is no pathway which is free and clear of the mirror that reflects *you* unto *you.* All of them have this reflection within them - all of them. As you come closer and closer in your understanding of soulmate, you will indeed have countenance with every aspect of that which be you. At times, and even now in your time, you emphasize a certain aspect of your Self that you would desire for that which be I, and for other entities, to perceive. This is alright. It is part of human nature. However, when unlimited God comes forth, all aspects are perceived and loved in the instant of perception. When you can do this with yourself, without even stopping to consider whether it is good or bad, *then you shall merge with the essence of your soul and go forth into eternal life called forever.*

Some of you judge according to what you call age: 'Oh, but this entity is so decrepit' - but this is judgment too. You know, heavy in age is beautiful, for it is heavy in wisdom, heavy in knowingness and experience, and indeed youthful - wondrously, experiential youthful in expression of divinity. A child indeed - why do they call it a second childhood? They come full circle. However, many of you do judge one another according to superficial outward characteristics. If you despise your neighbour and yet you say 'I love God', you do not understand the meaning of love, you do not understand the meaning of God. And this is alright. You shall. That is why you are experiencing it, so that you *can* know. When you all go forth with trumpets blaring from your heart, announcing indeed the coming of the Christus, when you go forth in this manner, and walk in wisdom in the ways of light, you shall indeed walk in the way of your soulmate.

Now, the experience of coming into the knowingness of your soulmate, be it female with female, female with male, or male with male - all can be soulmates - will occur when you can perceive and love every aspect of you that is disharmonious; for when you love it, you love that part of you that is reflected within the other entity. As you do this, you embrace humanity bit by bit by bit, facing over and over again aspects of you which you did not even know existed. You know, you learn the stuff you are made of when you rub elbows with your neighbours and when you rub fenders with them. The stuff you are made of is the stuff of God. When you understand this, you will understand what it is to experience your soulmate.

Flowers, and your animal kingdom, indeed they have soulmates. They were created of God, of the consciousness that is of the divine split, the separation. They are, as you, understood as electrums cast into coagulated matter with soul essence memory, with soul essence desire and divine thought. You created them in the expansion of density. Indeed, they align themselves unto your own desire and that is why you partake of them as foodstuffs. They align themselves into the service of that which created them. They are divine in their own essence and they shall come into the knowingness of their own sovereignty in super-consciousness when no thing shall devour them at all, and they do not devour one another either. In super-consciousness all things will partake of energy directly through the electrums of the atmosphere via the crown seal, and all shall be sovereign unto one another, allowing of one another. The lion shall indeed lie down with the lamb and all shall be at peace. Then indeed peace abides upon the land and the kingdom of heaven reigns supreme. You know, when they say that the kingdom of heaven lies within, it merely means that it lies within the essence that be you, the God essence of you in order to create it. You create it within and without, for you are of duality in physicality. The understanding of this creation is super-consciousness - the second coming of the Christ. This is the time of convergence of all the pathways coming into the One - all the different aspects of your own consciousness in a microcosmic understanding coming into the unified knowingness of the One - when indeed, woman reclaims her sovereignty and man reclaims his love, and they become balanced and in harmony yet again.

Many of you are finding yourself in a pickle jar and you are creating your own vinegar, but you know, you can create it as sweetness as well. Who says pickles have to be sour? Can they not taste as sweet as the peach? Your basketful of troublements can be viewed as sustenance, not as waste to be dispensed with. Your troublements are what allows you to understand *you*. Bless them - all of them. In blessing them, you bless your soulmate. The consciousness of your other essence [soulmate] in this particular personality Self is constantly feeding on your experience, and you on its - *constantly*, regardless of how you choose to experience. You stub your toe - that is an emotional experience called pain. It really matters not what it is, but if you align yourself with God, then indeed that is what your soulmate will experience as well. As they come forth from the heavens, from the inner Earth, from non-manifest reality into manifest reality, you will have countenance with them, and all of them will abide with you - all of them. You will embrace one another with tears streaming down your cheeks in recognition of that violet flame of you that has been ignited into the freedom called ascension, called immersion into the God I Am. As you come into this immersion, into an openness to Allness, you will *know* the Allness, including what you judge to be painful, what you judge as agony, as desolation, as bitterness and jealousy and hatred. You will bend your knees to the mirror of yourself and you will say unto yourself: 'I love you in all your resplendent and magnificent aspects.'

Coming into the knowingness and countenance of your soulmate is not like riding off into the sunset, you know? It is not a guarantee for happiness, for happiness is a choice of every moment. Happiness is not the result of your soulmate coming unto you to make it all better. Perhaps it is not the sunset, perhaps they take you to the twilight zone, but that is not what makes it all better for you in your life. *What makes the experience of life harmonious is you experiencing joy.*

What is a soulmate if it be not this? For indeed, all of you are soulmates of God. That is what it means when Christ takes God as a bride. The Christ of you merges with the God I Am and that is what you are experiencing in practical application this day of your time. That is also what is meant by 'physician heal thyself'. That is also what is meant by 'let your light shine forth'. All your literature, all your grand philosophies, all your grand teachings of spiritual nature have as their basis and foundation the knowing of the divinity of life. That is the core of soulmate.

There was a young woman who spoke to the entity of her choice: 'Do you not think you could fall in love with a girl like me?' And he said unto her: 'As long as you are not too much like me.' That is what you all say to yourself: 'As long as they are not too much like me, it is alright. As long as they are not like me, except in this area, then they can teach me a thing or two'. Does this sound familiar to anyone? 'They can be my complement' - is that not what 'opposites attract' means? But physical law does not operate in this manner. It abides in divine law and according to that *like attracts like.* The concept of opposites attracting one another is merely a superficial understanding, for it will attract initially. The recognition of that for which they search is not within them, because what they search for is that which be they. If it is opposite, it is not displayed in that particular resonance, and therefore, it is shortlived. There was another essence that came and said unto her mate: 'I do believe I am falling in love with you. I am already beginning to dread the divorce' - quite a statement about the consciousness upon your plane at this time. You have a hotel heart - always room for one more. You do! Upon this plane it is one across the other until you find your soulmate. 'If that one is not it, toss him. I'll try another'. I know your nature and I love you, and I jest with you because it is truth, and you understand it as truth. That is why you chuckle, because you know your nature too, and it is divine nature, for it is allowing you to understand humanity through light-hearted awareness. Capture the wisdom of it so that you may merge with this wisdom, not to be experienced outward of you, but to be captured of your breast, of your soul. Know it! Own it! When you do, it is not to be experienced again in physicality, and you go onward to grander adventures of God, if you choose, that is.

You search for love so desperately; for eons of time you have done so, in your literature, in your song, in your legend, in your ancient history, even before recorded history, there has been the fervent search for love. The woman has always been afraid of age, of being rejected, not wanted, unloved, for indeed, her hearth was within her man's breast. That was the key to her survival, but it is no more. The key to her survival is in the same place as his is - within her own breast. When she became heavy in age, she became in her estimation, worthless, valueless, and she carried even more soul memory unto the generations yet to come with the intensity of this knowing. The separation indeed increased and culminated in even further separation, in further density. You went as far as you could go into separation so that you may understand the turning point into the merging, from involution to evolution.

Now, age has indeed been a heavy piece of furniture upon your plane. It is because it has been given so much emphasis. The masters of your ancients - they knew beyond age, they knew beyond time.

Woman did not come into this knowing because she was not given validity to experience that wisdom in physicality. She is now, however, coming into her own resplendent Goddess awareness, and it is divine. It is indeed the vortex of transmutation through the alchemy of Christus coming forth, transmuting the base metal into the gold - the lower seals into the golden illumination of God, by allowing yourself to precipitate anything you desire simply by desiring it - divine thought energy made manifest. That is the era of God to be experienced. That is the era of soulmate to be experienced! In super-consciousness all will merge and have relationship with their soulmates - all of them. Those who do not, will not be partaking of super-consciousness.

When the merging of soulmates occurs in super-consciousness, the creation of life through the merging in physicality of the soulmate essence will occur through birthing without pain. The feminine will be opening up the petals of the rose in joy to allow new life to be born and then the petals will resume the bud yet again. The womb will become a place of life and joy and not of darkness and fear. Indeed, the soulmate experience in super-consciousness will merely be one God unto another. Do you know, when you understand your soulmate, you become *all* the frequencies. You do not say: 'Oh, that one has the vibes for me - must be my soulmate, I resonate', but you will resonate to all because you will encompass the entire spectrum of frequencies. You will become unlimited. Therefore, the soulmate family that you experience will incorporate the entirety of humanity. That is why I speak so fervently about loving of SELF and all others through SELF, because this is the ultimate soulmate union. Not one with another, but one with all, to become ONE.

Oh Romeo, the Casanova - he taught me well you know. But you know, when I was this Casanova (I may as well speak about me for a moment), I understood union and love abounding for the woman I was with. Joy of the moment, indeed, does this sound familiar? Joy of the moment experienced for the juice and flavour and savour of the preciousness of that joy, then off to the next one. That one was precious too, but I never gave promiscuously with my heart. I always gave earnestly. Could I help it if there was another beauty down the lane, hm? That was my thinking then. It is alright. I love that part of me that was the scallywag. I love that part of me that was human and limited, for it taught me much. It taught me to understand love, for I searched and I searched and I went through an entire dictionary of women and I still found not that jewel that I so fervently craved, that jewel of preciousness of femininity that was my ideal. It was not understood even after all those experiences. I really did understand in that life what it was to love God, and it was the assistance of my limitations that brought me into this knowingness. It was also the assistance of the limitations that I placed upon myself when I partook of facet after facet of that which I considered undesirable - in encountering others and loving them anyway, loving them without regard to what they presented outwardly.

I came to this knowingness at the close of that particular experience of life, and when I partook of the fruit of God, I became God, I understood love. Love not as you would understand it in a relationship upon the plane, the love that I had searched for and not found, but love that transcends any soulmate relationship. It is the love of SELF through all of life, the whole of life, including all the birds, all the insects, all the stars in the heavens, all the clouds which cover the mountaintops, all the leaves upon all the trees, all the rivulets which become the ocean, indeed all the grains of sand upon the desert.

As I gazed indeed into the nest of a loon and saw a new egg that was cracked, by the forces of nature, I did not perceive depravity, cruelty or tragedy. I perceived the beauty of a cracked egg, for within it was the understanding of uniqueness and divine creation. This was part of the experience that led me to understand what it is to perceive God, to behold God, and to know its Isness in everything - in the cracked egg, in the pain of relationships, in the sorrow of the search that indeed brought forth only emptiness. All of it was beauteous. There is no thing that is not beauteous, and in this beauty you shall know your soulmate. In this understanding you perceive the light called God, experienced as your soulmate, and you shall understand having a face to face love affair with yourself. Fall in love with yourself! Take yourself out to dinner, hm? Court yourself. How many of you have done this? Have you become enchanting to yourself, wooing yourself? Become respectful, in admiration, in honour and humility of SELF. How many of you have done this? This is what you would do to your soulmate, is it not? But your soulmate is *you*. Practice time, hm? When you can issue forth this sort of love to SELF - I speak not of arrogance, I speak of love with humility - then indeed your soulmate shall manifest to be experienced through you, for you exchange experiences unto one another. And it is always thus, whether you are incarnate together or whether you are in the 31st universe of a 5th density planet - you are still exchanging experiences, constantly.

In your slumber, many of you have had countenance with your soulmate essence, and your soulmate essence has had countenance with you. The dreams that come to you and do not make sense and you cannot figure them out - it is because you are experiencing across the boundaries of space and time with other aspects of SELF. It has meaning to you, for as you exchange knowingness and capture the wisdom, you become completed, whole, unified in Oneness.

There are those in this audience whose partner is their soulmate and those who have had countenance with a soulmate. This can be a very interesting situation indeed. To say that it is interesting suffices for now. 'Explosive' is the word. However, it is because you are faced with that part of yourself in the opposite gender, that you do not desire to encounter. Whatever bugs you most will come unto you because you have not embraced it within Self, and therefore it comes unto you to show it to you so that you may embrace it within yourself and merge into harmony and balance. Whatever it is that frustrates you - what do you call them, your pet peeves? - it will come unto you, for these are the limiters, the thorns which separate you from yourself, which prevent you from understanding the joy of you. When you can love these thorns, then harmony abides.

Questions and answers.

Q: St. Germain, do you mean that all experiences in our dream state are related to our soulmates?

All of them are an exchange in knowingness. Some of them are experiences with your soulmates, but all of them, regardless of what they are, bring wisdom to you. You see, there are more than two soulmates. There are two soulmates in the understanding of male soul essence energy and female soul essence energy, but within the male and within the female, there are multitudinous, alright?

Q: What about countenance with members of one's own soulmate family, with those of one's own gender? Do these experiences still go on?

Of course.

Q: So the experiences one could have with a soulmate of the opposite gender, one could also have with..

..with a soulmate of the same gender. Of course. Soulmate does not mean sexmate. Otherwise it would be called that.

Q: Why the thirteen families?

It is the understanding of the rays of the spectrum which are perceived in third density as coagulated matter. Therefore, thirteen is a very powerful number, for it is the Allness in physicality. Not the Allness in harmony with the God essence, but the Allness in the understanding of the manifested creation called Earth. Therefore, thirteen is to be found everywhere, even in your ancient records.

Adam and Eve in Genesis - it is a symbolic description of the division of Oneness, from androgeny, into male and female. They went forth and scattered their seed upon the Earth. Do you know what this means? They went forth and created out of the body of soulmate essence, the energy of multitudinous soul essences called male and female.

Q: What is the common thread, the resonance, within a soulmate family?

You will have resonance when you come into unlimitedness, but as long as you remain and abide within your physicality and the perceptions thereof, you will understand this resonance only with those aspects which you recognize as part of SELF, which you have gathered unto you in this reality. As you experience in other realities, it is a different frequency and it will gather different resonances unto it, until all come together as One.

Q: Does it happen often that soulmates of the opposite gender are born into this life experience in a similar year, or is there often a great age difference?

It depends upon the choice of the entities, my dear. It occurs in all manners of circumstance. There is no limited manner in which it has to occur. The God essence of you that chooses is unlimited. You may recognize a parent partaking of much doting and admiration of a sibling. Perhaps this is her soulmate, but she does not have an age consistency to experience it as an opposite gender relationship. You see?

Q: Yes, I understand. It does not work any particular way.

This is so. I will tell you this: Your soulmate will not take your pain away. *You* take your pain away, by choosing to be in harmony and in alignment, by choosing not to experience it as pain, but as joy. It is a choice.

Q: How does one recognize a soulmate?

That is a very popular question. How do you know your soulmate? Well, how do you know yourself? Would you recognize yourself if you met yourself in the hallway?

Q: I think so.

It is the same thing.

Q: So it is just someone who is so much like oneself..

You will feel a tugging of the heart. You will indeed feel the vibration stirring the emotion, like a grand ladle within your soul. The heart palpitations will begin, the breath will indeed quicken, the life energy force within you will pulsate at a higher frequency. You will recognize it in this manner, but do not be surprised if it is not your dream lover, if *you* are not *your* dream lover. I will tell you this: Many of you go forth in your parkways, strolling along on a summer day and you feel something in your breast, a stirring, a vibration - someone is there. You turn, and: 'Oh, but it is only a bedraggled old man.' Therefore, you cast your gaze away. 'Oh, it was nothing'. See how your judgments come at you? They are your teachers, likened unto that which be I, they reflect you to you.

Q: Are twin flames more like a companion of the soul?

It is an identical resonance reverberation of the same frequency within the different bodies of energy.

Q: Are many twin flames coming together now in this time?

Of course, because many Christ-consciousnesses are being born.

Q: To love what we do not like in ourselves, is to learn to love it within them, so we can love ourselves more?

Indeed, but it is not a pressure. It is a pleasure. As you come into countenance with your soulmates, you will find yourself in many perplexing situations. 'How did I get into this one?' You will find yourself quite emotional at times, because the emotions are coming forth so you may recognize and embrace them, all of them. Your tears will be streaming, your pain will rush forth - it is not only the convergence. It is your soulmates coming forth to merge with you in your light body. Indeed, your siblings, all of your relationships with your business houses - those are relationships too, all of these relationships are coming for you to garner the wisdom from them. They are indeed becoming close to your heart, surfacing as emotion, because it is there for you to tap. All you need do is prime the pump with love, and the waters of life will flow and flow and you will wonder how to turn it off at times. 'Is this not enough? When is it going to stop? How much can an entity take?' I hear you all say this from time to time, but when you judge the amount of it, you merely place yourself into further separation. Going with the flow of the waters of life is bringing forth more and more experience and you expand and expand eternally into the foreverness. You know what forever is? It is never-ending. It is so full, it cannot be understood. Your desire to stop the clock for a time, is your desire to judge and not love what is occurring. If you were really relishing it in your now moment, and in all wonderment of it, of course you would desire it to continue, for you would know it is beauteous. All of this is soulmate, and you thought we were coming here to discuss romance, but, you know, this is romance of the grandest nature. We are not romancing the stone, we are romancing the One, and the One is God.

Q: St. Germain, as one is falling in love so deeply with all of life, one is therefore falling in love with the soul essence of one's SELF in all of life.

Of course.

Q: And then the soulmates manifest in the moment, non-physical or physical, is that correct?

Of course. *When you dispense with the idea of soulmate as an entity who will bring you happiness and understand soulmate as the rest of humanity, then the entity, the soulmate, who will allow you the experience of happiness, will appear.* It is a dichotomy, a grand paradox of life, but this is how it works in your reality.

Q: I am a little confused about the difference between a soulmate and a twin flame. I understand that a twin flame is your exact frequency totally, but then a soulmate is just part of that?

The body of energy of you that is of femaleness has within it many different diversions of frequencies of the spectrum of light. As the one particular frequency which you perceive as yourself, has a resonance, there is a corresponding resonance in the male body of energy. This is your twin flame. All the rest of them are your soulmates. The two of them together ignite one another and transmute into wholeness and will bring all of them together.

Q: This resonance stays with me no matter how..?

In this life experience you understand your twin flame as a particular frequency vibration. Indeed you may come into light and raise this vibration into a higher resonance, but when you do this you expand the horizon of vibrations. It is not a changing. It is a merging - an addition if you will. You see? That is called becoming enlightened, becoming in light of. Adding more of your light unto you so that you are increased and expanded. You see?

Q: St. Germain, it is not necessarily true that if one is in physicality, that one's twin flame be in physicality as well, right?

This is so. 'Where oh where be my soulmate again'. You are in hot pursuit.

Q: Exactly, I am waiting for the doorbell to ring now.

Remember the knob of the door is on the inside. You open the door unto your soulmate by opening the door unto you.

Q: What about when they are the same gender in physicality? Is that possible?

Of course. Of course, you call it brethren. Many of you call it identical twins that are inseparable. When one passes this plane into a different reality, the other follows, for indeed they experience a void within their heart. They have felt that they have lost a part of themselves, therefore, they go to the reality to which their soulmates went. They will experience in this manner until they realize they are of wholeness unto themselves. Always following one another, always in search of. As long as you are a seeker, you will become the master teacher of how to be a seeker. Many times I wonder what it is that you seekers would do if you ever found it. You would have no hobby anymore.

Q: St. Germain, could you speak about your twin flame and possibly give us an idea of some of the incarnations she might have had?

She has had several counterparts in physicality and many in non-physicality. The counterparts in history are resplendent. The mother principle of life in Egypt - Isis. The water bearer, the understanding of life to supplicate, to nurture, to nourish and buoy and indeed support all who come within her waters. She had experience in this nation (U.S.A.). A grand entity was she. She placed together very tenderly your grand banner. She was in Atlantis, Egypt, Greece, and Israel.

Some of her names are not recorded. This is alright. She experienced very much humility of life, and barrenness at times. She understood poverty, pain and sacrifice, the ultimate love. She participated in bringing forth the seed of Abraham into the land of Israel. She participated with King David. She once was of a harem. No name of history, but grand and loved by all. I will tell you this: When I came upon her countenance, I was smitten, but I did not know why. Her hair was glistening in the golden sun, soft like a newborn babe. Her countenance was sweet like a melon, and her cheeks were like the blush of a rose. Her breath was honeysuckle, and indeed her touch was like the touch of God. She giggled and laughed like a child at play. She romped in the vineyards. That is where I met her, and you wonder why I have such a desire for the ruby, hm? She nurtured the vines and the clusters with loving caresses like they were her own children, and I fell in love with a beauteous vision of God. I took her hand and I wept. I was on my knees in the dirt, the earth of the land, and I wept because I was in such adoration of the beauty that be she.

Do you know what she said unto me, grand teacher that she was? 'But you know, I am your mirror.' That was the first time I heard that one. Grand teacher, womankind is wondrous, and they teach the male essence how to love, how to allow and how to give God I Am of themselves. You know, I have had embodiment as a woman, but I have never born children. That is a gift of life that is precious indeed, a gift that is incomparable - to bring forth life spontaneously, creatively, supportively, in the manner that you create with your own flesh and blood that which is flesh and blood. You know, I experienced love in a way I had never experienced before, and I knew my soulmate because I understood myself.

This was after those days of my roguishness, my rascalry, and I had understood the longing and yearning for love. But I held not within my breast that I be requited, and I found a precious jewel that was ever-giving, ever-allowing, ever-loving. I merged with her in soul essence and I became God. It was shortly after the countenance with her that I wept in the meadow and beheld God in the sunrise and I came to know ascension. I did not merge with her physically because the preciousness of life was beyond physicality in that point of the ripeness of my soul essence.

Q: St. Germain, is it possible for one soulmate to wish to be with another soulmate and that the other does not want to be in that light?

I understand of which you speak. In that case that soulmate desires to experience that particular reality. You see, there is divinity in all experience so it is not to be seen as a limitation, for it allows grand knowingness. Perceiving and receiving the vibrations of your soulmate without physical union - without countenance of romantic nature - occurs so that you may know your soulmate of opposite gender in all facets of experience, and to gain the knowing of *you* in totality - that which is platonic and that which is not. You know, it is a grand puzzlement that they call that platonic, because Plato was not.

Your siblings are grand reflectors in purity and clarity in the experience of the soulmate essence of you. They will directly come unto you and say: 'Oh, but mother, why did you do that?' And you have to face yourself all of a sudden. Perceive the wisdom that they give you from their hearts, from the purity of their being, receive it, relish it and love them for the gift they give you. Admonishing them because you were embarrassed only allows further separation. Let them know the beauty and gift they give unto you, for the knowingness you have understood. The children who are coming forth upon super-consciousness of the land at this time will all be bearing gifts for you; more than the pearls of wisdom of the ages from the masters, for they will contain all the jewels in the treasure chest of themselves. All you need do is scoop it up and express gratitude unto them for the divine sharing they exhibit. They come here for this purpose, not to be restricted or limited into further separation, but to be freed into the unity of Oneness - to be freed into the wisdom that they contain within their own breast.

As you suckle your siblings, bring forth the gift of love within your milk and you will be giving back to them what you have received. The gift of love within the sustenance they receive is the gift of life, the gift of regeneration. It is the forever flow of life. They will have a particular preference for violet at this time, for they are merging their maleness and femaleness and that is what violet is. They are becoming not child of female or child of male, but child of God. Do not chide them because of their androgeny. Love them for their unity, and mirror from them your own unity.

I will allow you a brief respite. There are certain rumps that are numb. Partake heartily and rejuvenate yourself with each other. Soulmate unto another. Alright? So be it.

(After the respite.)

Greetings beloveds. Did you gaze unto one another with the knowingness that you were gazing unto yourself? Indeed, as I gaze unto you, I see your many hues. Beauteous, they all are. Resplendent and resonant, they all are. That which is spoken unto you this day is verbiage. It is to satisfy your Alter Ego that you are getting something, but what is really given unto you is of the heart and it is not spoken. What I give to you is not of words. You may partake of the words and philosophical knowledge. You may partake of what is given to you of the heart and thus partake of the resonance of God that is identified of you.

The male/female essence of you - some have called it the ying/ yang - it is not *in* you. The femaleness or maleness of you does not abide *in* you. *It is you!* It is not within you, it is of you. It is the duality in totality. In other words, it is male or female in your resplendent exemplification of physicality and it is male and female as God realized in physicality.

Now, a twin flame is a frequency identical to another frequency within the same body of energy; but you know, that is only according to one frequency. It is the same for all the frequencies. So you have multitudinous twin flames. A twin flame for this one, a twin flame for this one, and for this one, according to all the resonances that abide within your soulmate energy body of maleness or femaleness. So does that perplex you a bit? When all the twin flames are ignited into the violet flame of freedom, they come forth into the One, in union with the totality, the crowning glory of the God I Am.

So, this fervent search for your twin flame has opened a few doors here, because as you blend into all the frequencies and become more unlimited, so does your twin flame, and they become resplendent of all the frequencies. So where does that leave you in your desperate search, as you seek out the other entity whose company would be your pleasure? And what about the shortcomings of this entity? You know, it is not the shortcomings, it is the longstayings, but if they abide long enough, you shall learn to love them. I come unto you and bless you with the reflection of you and I understand why you are here and I come forth so that *you* may understand why you are here. Your search is over. The journey is indeed a grand adventure that is forever. It does not stop. The adventure is life and the search is contained within every now moment and the relishment of it.

Now, the merging of the soulmate essences of all of this, of the solar system, of universes, is bringing forth the Christus on this planet. Microcosmic into macrocosmic. You merge the soulmate essences of your flora and your fauna and your minerals. They have soulmates too, you know, and you wonder why you always have a tendency to place one crystal next to another. Now, these merge in their essences and consciousnesses and become clarified of one another and in understanding of one another. As this occurs, the consciousness called humanity shall do likewise and as this occurs, the consciousness that is of planetary and stellar understanding shall come into the same formation, into unified wholeness; so shall all the universes. What does this mean, hm? Your planets will ascend. Your stars will ascend. Your universes will go forth into ad infinitum frequency. Grand puzzle here - what happens if everything ascends? Everything!

This occurrence represents the completion of the cycle of you as manifesting Gods in physicality. You will merge into the Source, which is merely another microcosm, for it is a Source within a Source within a Source within a Source, and you shall begin the grand adventure, yeah, all over again in a different reality. Does that sound exciting, creating a new prehistory all over again? That is an unlimited statement. Why? Why do we need to do that? You do not need to, but it is the desire of the God that contemplated itself in the first place and created your experience of creation and desires to expand into further creation, for it is constantly expansive, increasing and ever-unlimited into further awareness of SELF.

Q: Oh, so we do not have to do this over again?

Not in this reality, a different one, something you cannot even imagine with your finite mind. It will go forth yet again into a different manner of manifestation that is not even of electrums and electromagnetic understanding and light, something entirely different. Your finite mind blows a fuse when you try to contemplate this, for it only understands within the confines of its nature, that is electrums and light. To be God is to be on-going. You know, another statement is: To be God is to be unGod, and that is man. When man becomes God yet again, he has birthed Christus and has expanded the God I Am. Infinity - you know it does go in the other direction as well.

The atoms within your embodiment are soulmates of one another. There are universes existing within a molecule. There are soulmates existent within that. This is infinity into the opposite polarity of expansion. When you contemplate yourself in this respect, does it really matter if you had a quarrel with your neighbour?

Now, what about siblings born of soulmates? Are they soulmates or not? They have the same genetic memory; do they also have the same soul memory? Indeed, yes, but of a different vibration. It is of the same soul essence. When twin flames merge [sexual union], the life that issues forth from them is begotten of the same frequency. Therefore, it is indeed a powerful Trinity. 'I am the way, the truth and the light'. That is what is spoken when this Trinity abides. Jeshua was born of soulmates, of twin flames. He ignited the Christ-consciousness of his soul essence and during his tender years, his puberty, during his sojourn to the land of Egypt, the land of Tibet and China, he was christed because he allowed the Christus to come forth in a realized understanding. This occurred in the area of Egypt, which is a vortex of power, the origin point of this planet. The Christus was born of this planet in the same manner that mankind was born of this planet.

Did you know that mankind was placed upon the planet in the same area and later migrated to the fertile area of Mesopotamia? That is another tale for telling. Quite an interesting one also.

The union of soulmates issues forth Christus. That is not for you to go around hurry scurry to find an entity to beget with so that you may have a Christ born in your household; but it is for you to know that grand, grand, grand events occur in your life when you partake of the love of SELF so that it may be reflected in the other essence of SELF that comes unto you in physicality.

Now, the siblings born of soulmates on this plane will be leading humanity into the era of super-consciousness. Some of them will be child prodigies; indeed, grand masters, youthful of heart and of tender body, but indeed heavy in knowingness, which is really light. These youngsters, as you call them, will lead you into freedom. They will teach you how to be young again, how to play again, how to live again. Take heart of them, and as you partake of their knowingness, partake of your own. Become the child again. Become the youngster that knew not limitation, that knew not frustration and heaviness of burden, that knew not pain and tears and bitterness and hatred and resentment. Become the child of you that loves, that is in wonderment and awe of everything, that is amazed at even a butterfly. Listen with your soul to these entities, for you will be listening to the soulmates of a new age.

Now, as I speak, the words are going in one ear and out the other from time to time, but they go in your heart and out unto your soulmate's heart. The vibrations are between the lines, so even if you are not listening, you are listening. Even when you are dreaming, and you call upon an entity to have companionship with you, in brotherhood, love, fellowship and communion, your soulmate also receives communion. You are nurturing one another, always. If you feel unloved, go into the deepest recesses of your imagination and allow yourself to partake of the chalice of love that is offered unto you by your soulmate essence, for it shall be requiting and refreshing. You shall be rejuvenated and renewed indeed. You shall come forth yet again full to the brim with love and happiness to give it unto the Earth plane, and the whole of the universe, so that it shall be given back to you.

Soulmates. Godmates. Why is there such a mystique about this? Why has there been for eons such a yearning for that which be outward of you to satisfy a particular longing of human nature? It is part of the separation factor that was understood of God when God contemplated itself to come into density, to experience physicality. There is nothing wrong with this longing. It is divine. It is part of your creation. So blessed be it, but know indeed, that although you embrace it and love it, it need not be considered painful. It can be joyous in the knowingness of what it is. Transmute it into joy. You may do this in any moment with anything you experience. Remember the pickle jar I spoke about - you can also make it sweet.

Do you recall that I said your soulmates are all the different bodies of energy that resonate to their corresponding frequencies, both in physical and non-physical dimensions of experience? Now what is this but simultaneity and multi-dimensionality? When I speak about your multi-dimensional Selves, those essences of you that are on other planes of demonstration, immersed in different consciousnesses of different vibrations, impart to you their wisdom as you allow it. These are your soulmates, the other you's. Some of you do know where different aspects of yourselves are, but it really matters not where they are in location, or in space and time. The dimensionality of it does not matter. What matters is that you know what you are desiring to know; not that you know about it, but that you know it. And knowing it is knowing *you*. Many of you will say: 'But that particular character - I do not have that within me. It is not in me to be a slayer. It is not in me to be a judge or a persecutor.' I beg of you to take another look at yourself. How can you understand what it feels like and the wisdom contained within, to be the persecutor if you have not experienced it, in one manner or another? It does not have to be physical. To capture upon the tapestry of your soul this wisdom, you must experience the emotion of it. Much of this is what your soulmate does, all the different essences of it. You are a fragment of that essence, and your experiences contribute to your soulmate's and theirs to yours. So whenever I speak of your multi-dimensional Selves, I am speaking of your soulmates. All of them are really twin flames unto one another.

Now, there are many of you who haunt the taverns, the spiritual places, who haunt those places they feel their soulmate may be abiding in. I speak not only of the opposite gender, but someone that you can have communion with and have a love relationship with, through identity. You know, my dearest brothers and sisters, as you search in this manner, you search for that which does not exist, for if you do not recognize it within yourself, you cannot recognize it outside of yourself.

Now, what you desire to have reflected back unto you - what you are yearning for above and beyond all else - is your impetus for life. If you understand what that is, then you shall manifest it for yourself. It is being in love with yourself, having a romance with yourself; providing yourself with unconditional love, looking beyond what would be judged as flaws in the heart and core of you. You are the apple of God's eye. Have a relationship with the God of All, the divine essence within all. Participate with nature, for it is also your lover. Understand the wind as it dances and tickles the blades of grass and reveals capriciously the silvery underside of an emerald leaf. Let it kiss your cheek and whisper the wisdom of the ages unto your ear and into your heart. Indeed, the wind is a grand lover. It tosses sand into your eyes from time to time to afford you the embrace of irritation as well. The wind is the breath of life. Your Mother Earth breathes upon you the wind in her storms and in her calming seas as well. Learn also to appreciate the gales and hurricanes of your life; for it is not the gale, it is the set of the sail that gives you direction. The set of the sail is your perception. It indeed is wondrous and you will learn to perceive the whole of life - all the entities who you come into contact with - observing them as the wind, as beauteous, as airy, as characteristic of life itself. They are a grand mirror, a grand teacher to you. The wind in the willows whispers to your soul, if you will listen, the sounds beyond the silence. If you will listen to the heartbeat of the Earth, you will hear the heartbeat of your soulmate, for indeed, your soulmate participates in the consciousness of the Earth, the consciousness of the universes. That 'wind' illustrates it unto you all the time, but you ignore it, and therefore, you ignore your soulmate. 'Oh, but this is not important. I have much business to attend to. See here, look at my agenda.' The wind can wait. It has been abiding for millenia. It does not mind abiding. You are the one that is in urgency of knowing the essence of the wind which is also the essence of the mate of your being, which is the essence of God.

You see, you search and search and when it comes to you, you perceive it to be a no-thing. You understand it not. When Jeshua came unto this plane, he said unto the entities about him: 'Go forth. You are made in the image of your maker.' That was the knowing of divinity, and he also said unto these same entities: 'Look unto your brethren, for they are God', and: 'Love is of the heart, find it therein.' Not thereout! *Therein* - but the entities did not understand. The words went into the holes of their ears and back out again.

You harness your would-be lovers with a rope of enslavement, likened unto a lasso, and place them in the chain gang, as it were, and bid them do duty. 'This is what a lover should be - if you love me you will do this. Oh, but you should not have done this.' This is not love, my dear brothers and sisters. Love is unconditional. It allows, regardless of the 'shoulds' and 'should nots' on your plane. Love is indeed the expression of emotion of God. I spoke to you of emotion, all the emotions of pain, of heartbreak, of anger and bitterness, of compassion and humility, joy and ecstasy. But you know, these are the emotions of man the Christus created to experience God-man in physicality. The emotion of God I Am, the divine creative essence within all of you, is indeed love. Raise that vibration one octave and you have joy. When you merge all the emotions together into a grand melting pot, and raise the vibrations one octave, you will have joy. This means that anger, bitterness, hatred, jealousy, greed and pettiness, are all merely infant love. They have not matured as yet.

So do not cast a judgmental eye upon these emotions of yourself. Love them. Bring them into maturity. Understand them as contributing to the stew of you. Many times it is quite a stew. That is alright. All the seasonings are bringing forth their own special flavour. The flavour of pepper alone can be quite interesting - considered at times to be undesirable, hot for the palate and for the seat at times - but the flavour of pepper given in harmony and balance can contribute a divine aspect to the pot of you. Loving yourself through all these emotions will enable you to love yourself through the thick and thin of it, the broth and the gravy.

Understand the grasshopper as *you*. Understand the sky at night as *you*. See *your* face in the moon's face. They are all *you*. They all reflect *you*. When you understand this, you will also understand that all of this is your soulmate as well. The grains of sand, the purple hue of the mountains at dusk, the notes of the loon in the morn, the beams that fall across the lake from the moon and cast a glancing eye unto lovers snuggled underneath a bush in an embrace - indeed, all of this is *you*. You created it all by your magnificent divine essence. The God I Am within you desired to experience the Earth plane, to understand creation and manifestation, to experience the dimension of physicality.

The pearls of wisdom carry forth with it justice forever. You know what justice forever is? It is jubilance, joyousness and playfulness; splashing in the puddles of life, dancing in the rain, spinning and whirling around without concern for space or time. Concern for life having to be a certain way is your judgment. Allow it to be as it is and be happy regardless of how it is. Allow the others to be judgmental, if they choose to, but the understanding of happiness and joy and non-judgment is a choice, not a result! You have this choice every now moment as it presents itself unto you. Now after now after now you may choose joy after joy after joy. Release the slave-driver time and you immerse yourself in this now moment and you will find yourself free. Justice comes as the balance. Opening your breast to the Earth, to the experience of life, regardless of how it presents itself to you, without judgment, is vulnerability. And what is vulnerability? Allowing your heart to be penetrated by the arrows of Eros, and you are indeed the one with the bow. You may pierce your own heart with divine love for yourself and in doing so, you do it for all of humanity. Pierce your breast with this knowing and you pierce the multi-dimensional aspects of your soulmates and you will find yourself in another dimension, for you will have pierced the time continuum into forever. That is ascension. That is what some call the rapture. That is God realized. Come into an experience of passion, kindle a grand blaze, indeed bask in the bonfire of it. Warm your frigid back in its caresses. Understand that it is indeed powerful and transforming, but it is also nurturing and loving. As you merge with that fire, that wondrous illumination of Godness, Isness - the presence of the creative force - you will be walking hot coals in your life; but if you know not judgment, they will not be hot.

The hot coals are the pressurized experience of your life, perceived as the divine fever. Many of you have heard of this. Your ancient writings tell you about divine fever. It is an experience of temperature rising, a chemical reaction of your embodiment. When the energy penetrates the crown seal of your body, you merge with the other essences who are you, your soulmates, and you will feel electrified with much more energy than you are accustomed to. Your body will change and transform to accommodate this energy. The neurons within your body will change. Your spinal column will develop into two, for indeed the polarities will balance in many aspects. Negative and positive will both be coursing through your spine. The overload of the pituitary gland as it distributes chemicals within your system, will be experienced as an ache of the head, but it is overload. It is the alarm button. It is the red flasher. As it buzzes, and you fill your belly with medication, you will notice another transformation yet, for when there is an overload of nature's provision, there is always another doorway, another opening. So nature's provision for this overload is to channel the energy into a gland that has not been used for eons of your time and that is the pineal gland, and it opens and blossoms of itself. Your pineal gland will effect a temperature rise, for it will distribute even more chemicals throughout your system. The brain is a receiver. It is an instrument. It is not where you abide, but it is indeed a grand instrument bringing forth the energy to enable your embodiment to change.

As you notice the aches and pains as they progress within your embodiment, it is new energy introduced into your system that you are not accustomed to and therefore it is perceived as subtle and vague aches and pains. It is aligning your organs. Some of them will be dissipating. Some of them will indeed be increasing and expanding, like your heart. The chambers will become non-divided and you will find your blood pressure changing as well. The distribution system of your body in regard to foodstuffs is in transition as well. At times you will have a certain amount of indigestion, for it is aligning itself to *not* digest the foods that are of heavier energy, because in super-consciousness you will not partake of foodstuffs at all. You will have direct access to the energy within your atmosphere and it will be accessed whenever there is a void in your system. A vacuum is created and the flow flows. Water shall be partaken of, but not foodstuffs.

These shifts and changes within you become even more accelerated than they are already, and this is also occurring in your soulmates. They notice these shifts and some of them are confused about it although they do not reside in the physical, because even in a non-physical manifestation they perceive changes although they are subtle; they are still changes in frequencies, in energy. Therefore, *as you come into the Oneness, it is of necessity that your soulmate does also.* It is a natural progression. Some of you will perceive the beauty of a magnificent, wondrous evening of your time, and as you breathe in the spice of autumn, the perfume of your summer, the musk of life about you, you will suddenly feel exhilarated, joyous, buoyant, desirous to give unto the Earth plane all there is, all the love of you, all the God of you. You know, when you experience this, your soulmate does too. This is the passion for life. This is indeed the zest of experiencing in physicality, but passion in physicality is also divine and valid.

The sexual merging with your physical soulmate is accorded to those entities who are not searching for it outwardly, and who are indeed unfolding into further unlimitedness.

As you exchange physically passionate energies with these entities, you will be exchanging with yourself, illuminating yourself. The explosion, the culmination of this exchange will come into a beautiful display of fireworks for you, for indeed, that is the explosion of God, that is the understanding of the spectrumized versions of you all coming together to experience epic ecstasy.

So, do not judge passion in the physical sense. It is not necessary to force yourself into celibacy to become One with God. For forcing anything indicates resistance, and if there is resistance in your consciousness, then it is not aligned and attuned to joy. I will tell you that the non-necessity for physical merging will come naturally in time, and that will bring you into ascension and non-physicality. It is a natural progression. It is understanding the passion for *all* of life, not merely experiencing only one aspect of a frequency to participate with. The desire to participate with another entity that is of your soul essence is divine, but it is not to be found out there. It is to be found in the heart. Look in the mirror. There are times when you look in the mirror and you see subtle changes and differences within the reflection. You are seeing your soulmate. You are seeing another aspect of yourself that is abiding in another dimension in that now moment. You will also see this in your dream states, in your slumber. Recognize that everything about you is a grand mirror, even inanimate objects. They are also your mirror, for you have created them and they reflect an aspect of you, otherwise they would not exist.

You know, your soulmate is not *like* you. It *is* you. When you know of your soulmate, it represents itself in your physiology. There is a blush upon the cheek, a sigh in the breast and you are all representing that understanding of the physiological changes within you. You are becoming enlightened, in light of, in knowingness of. As you reach out and touch one another with your hearts, with your souls, with your love, you are embracing the universe. Embrace it heartily, for it is indeed the garden of God.

In the allness, limitation and non-limitation are not understood as separate, but as Oneness. Gaze into the mirror of life, and I mean *all* of life. The grass before you is part of life, understand it as your soulmate, understand it as an essence of God that comes forth to merge with you in essence, and when you do this, you will experience divine love. When you experience this alignment and attunement with the All-That-Is, *your soulmate will manifest in physicality as a natural progression,* for you have aligned unto its occurrence. It will be birthed. The two flames will merge as One and they will ignite into the birthing of the Christus of you.

Now, you all may go forth into the density of life and your concerns and consternation about your daily activity, and your currency and the heaviness of it all. Then you will not be remembering consciously the understanding that I have given forth, but even the metal bird that honks is of the Christus. Without judgment it is as divine and valid as that which is a placid, serene meadow. Density is divine because it was created from the God of you, from the grand creative force. Do not judge an entity that does not abide by the timepiece. Do not judge this, for their life is the divine manifestation created by their own heart's desire. When you live in constant non-judgment, you live in the love that was illustrated by Jeshua, the Christus. Therefore, I say to you, go thou and do likewise. Give a flower of love to the whole of life and you will be giving the flower of love to your soulmate. *When this essence comes unto you in physicality, the two of you will flower and blossom.*

It is difficult for many of you to understand creation. It is not outward of you or separate from you. It *is* you. It is not a thing to gaze upon. It is a thing to be. When you consider God as being represented *as you,* then you will create gardens wherever you go - even in your concrete jungles, for life will flourish about you, always. Then, when you go into your marketplace, you will carry with you an aura of golden about you, and those you pass will turn to gaze upon you, for their souls have been touched by something in the desire to know and indeed, their soul was touched by the Christus of you. As you walk among the peoples of the land without saying any of your verbiage or giving forth grand teachings in any manner or other, you may touch them, all of them, with the rose of your heart, and they will become illumined by your presence.

Do you hear the wind speaking to you? Do you hear the water as it laughs merrily along its way, as it bounces like a child around the rocks and slides down the steep cliffs of life? There is life all about you if you will but perceive it, and the life is the love of God. You are embraced by it all the time. You need not have such fervent desire to seek a dream lover, for the dream lover is life and it is embracing you constantly. Allow yourself to be nourished and nurtured, caressed and embraced, *for the life of God is the love of soulmates. As you walk with one another, you are walking in the heart of God.* You need not search for love. You are loved, and if you will recognize that and perceive that you already embody the principle of love, you will become at peace. *Then you will merge with your soulmates and the merging of soulmates creates miracles.*

We are all a family. Your family is not only comprised of those that abide with you, but those that love with you. Be in love with this family. Join hands with them and be in communion and brotherhood and fellowship with the humanity that you call mankind. For indeed, peace will reign only when love reigns, and love reigns supreme in the kingdom of God.

There are those of you who contemplate maleness and femaleness as a gender. It is not a gender. It is a consciousness, although in physicality your polarity is represented as your gender, but the essence of the gender is a consciousness. It is a knowingness in and of itself. When you come into the knowing of the opposite gender *within* you, you will be at ease with *you* in the opposite gender, as it presents itself outward of you. When woman exhibits sovereignty, God power, she is allowing herself to drink of the cup of her soulmate in the opposite, that which is called male. When a man experiences softness and humility and love unlimited, he is drinking of the cup of his soulmate and partaking of the wisdom and knowingness therein.

As they merge together closer and closer and drink more and more of one another's cups, they become One, and they become one another's strength and one another's love.

In this manner, woman, the fourth density understanding of woman, will be strong and powerful and loving and allowing. So also shall be the man, both in harmonious balance with one another. There will be no difference except the polarity represented by the embodiment. So, if you are a man, do not be concerned whether you are too feminine, exhibiting love and softness and compassion, or whether you are too masculine if you are a woman, exhibiting sovereignty and power, for you are becoming balanced. Appreciate physicality. The passion of man and woman together - when it is given with love and alignment to the God I Am of each of you - it is not decadent. It is life. Even decadence is life when you perceive it without judgment.

You are really magnificent, you know? All of you are soulmates. Have you ever considered, in your fervent search for your soulmate, that your soulmate is in fervent search of *you?* Have you considered that it is a vice versa situation as well? You are the burning dream lover of someone else. That someone else will at times be surprised when you come along, for they do not consider that it is you that they are calling unto them. There is much to be said about love at first sight. For one thing, it saves a lot of time. Experience unconditional love at first sight, always, with everyone. When you do this, you will not need to look twice, for in the very first glance you will know GOD. Cupid shoots his bows in odd fashions these days, not considering age, creed, race, colour, culture or even that which is understood as human.

Hear the wind of silence whisper to you, for the many voices within you will be merged into the one knowingness of silence. There will not be a chatter in your consciousness, always urging you to do this thing or the other. You will follow the silence of your heart's desire. Your rudder will be set in knowingness and indeed, the crest of the wave will be quiet. You will ride the high tides of life and the stormy seas of life in silence. But when you are too busy with your third density concerns to notice the divinity within these concerns, all you hear is chaos and confusion and din of sorts. And this is alright, for indeed, there is divinity even in the confusion, but understand the silence in the confusion, the quietude in the chaos. All the voices that are about you resonate. The resonance is movement - not noise. The vibration is the vitality of God. It is not utterance. It is utter silence. Love is quiet.

There are those who you love, but you do not tell these entities that you love them. They have to squeeze it out of you. It is of the ripeness of time to spread love as well as light. Entities you dare not tell that you love them, *tell them*. You will create a vibration of unity that did not exist before. Those entities who make you tremble and quiver in your stockings, tell them that you love them. Go forth and give bountifully. Present it as a gift of your heart to everyone you encounter. Who knows? One of them may be your soulmate. When you do this, you will be surrounded by universal support.

The words I give unto you this day of your time, you may forget, for they are really the meaningless part, but you have been transformed, because you have come into an awareness, a newness of knowing that you did not have before. You will go hence from here, different somehow in a way that you cannot put your finger on. Your buttons have been pushed, the buttons of God love, Godmate, soulmate.

Q: St. Germain, by counterpart, is that another word for soulmate or twin flame?

Both. One is merely an emphatic version of the other.

Q: Germain, is my twin flame on the Earth plane?

In the Earth plane.

Q: In the Earth plane - inner Earth?

Oh but you know, my dearly beloved, those that are above the Earth plane come unto the Earth plane all the time. So do those who are within the Earth plane, who are of middle Earth, but they do not come quite as frequently as the space brothers.

Q: So he will be coming here, or I will be going there?

That is according to your own choosing.

Q: So I can manifest whatever I choose.

Indeed, you both can.

Q: Do you have his telephone number? I am jesting.

There are some of you to whom I could give phone numbers. I hear your readiness, but it would not do any good, you know, because when you meet them, you will judge them - because you judge yourself. It is not of the ripeness of time for you to have their countenance yet, or you already would.

I so desire to tell you the things you want to know. I so desire you to have your heart's desire and your heart's desire is to go forth into peace and love and to merge with the All-That-Is, to come into super-consciousness. It is not really to have your soulmate's address.

Q: St. Germain, could you review a little about twin flames?

Your twin flame is the identical vibration of the vibration you emit in your personality Self in this your now moment. As you become the Christus, you take on all the other frequencies of the original thirteen bodies of soul essence energy. They come unto you and the different frequencies together culminate in One. In this manner, there is more than one frequency abiding within you. In this manner, there is more than one frequency that would be an identical twin flame, and they are really all one twin flame, as the One comprises all, very much like the cells of your body, they form tissues and organs, bundles of like frequencies - the twin flames - but they are all part of the one body. It is all very simple. You are God. What else is there? You are the ones who complicate it into soulmates and twin flames and the like.

Q: So twin flames would be perfect mirrors for each other and soulmates would be too, but it would be just a different..

A different spectrum, indeed. A different understanding of yourself. Your organs are all for different purposes, created for different resonance reasons, for without the organs, the embodiment would not operate. In the same manner, without the multiplicity of the twin flames, the wholeness of the One flame would not be harmoniously understood. You see? It would not be in wholeness of itself.

The cells of your body which make up the organs are very much like the personalities of you. There are many of you and you all comprise different twin flames. So when you consider the wholeness of you as a soul body essence energy, there are many more than you could ever have in your bed. I beg of you to remember also that your soulmate is not always of the opposite gender. You do have soulmates of the same gender.

Q: But if there are lots and lots, why do they call it twin?

Twin means two. You see, when you have a male body essence energy, the female frequency that is of exact identical resonance is the twin flame. As each male resonates to a female, they are all twins to one another. When all these twins merge together as One, you have no separation anymore. Do you understand? We are speaking of unlimited horizons here.

Q: St. Germain, so does that mean that each of the original thirteen separations from the Source has an exact opposite polarity?

Exact likeness in opposite polarity.

Q: And that is why we have thirteen soulmates?

The twelve is illustrative of the twelve vibrations of colour, and the thirteenth is the understanding of the white - the Oneness - where all twelve come together to merge as One, but it is also perceived and known in density. In your colonies there were twelve states and one commonwealth. There were twelve disciples and Jeshua. It is illustrated everywhere. It is the same also with your soul body essence energy. Mankind has made things so difficult for itself to comprehend and causes itself a lot of confusion. This is divine, for it brings forth wisdom. However, the confusion is not necessary. All you need is the simplicity of life. All you need is God I Am and you have it all. All this other 'willy frilly' is not necessary. When you understand God I Am, you automatically understand all the rest.

I love you all so grandly. You do not understand this yet, but you are all my soulmates, and I bow unto you as I come unto you this day of your time. It is indeed an honour to participate with you in this manner, an honour of God. Each of you has a crown upon your head, unrealized God that you are, you do not know it is there, but it is, and I take off my crown to you in honour of the crown that you wear.

Beloved you all are, beloved indeed, of yourself and of that which be I. I am never away from you, any of you. I am always with you even unto the ends of the Earth.

I have given you the flame of freedom of my heart. I have given you my all. I love you all in the wholeness that you do not even know that you are. I am here to represent unto you that which you already are. I am here to give you my heart, my dearly beloved soulmates. I am here to open my heart unto you, for you to walk into it and know that it is your own, and the chambers therein are the cathedrals of celestial choirs. I AM I AM! Love is the emotion of God, and I love you - all of you. I love you more than you can even conceive of the word love. I love you enough to allow you to experience your life, however you choose. I judge you not, for how can I judge myself? How can you judge God? I love you to the ends of all the universes and all the grains of sand. I give you my heart. I give you the all of me, and when you are troubled or searching, frustrated or lonely, take it into your breast as your own and it will supplicate you and give you balm and allow you to know the peace that you desire. *I am simply your brother who comes unto you and loves you, to share with you, to reflect unto you your own knowingness, to love you back unto yourselves so that you may love others in like manner. And when you do this, the physical expression of your soulmate automatically appears. It appears to pop out of the air and at times it really does.*

Do you know how much of an honour it is to come to you in this manner? It is indeed a miracle. Farewell, my beloveds. Namaste.

Chapter 3

SPIRITUALITY AND SEXUALITY

Greetings my brothers and sisters!

Indeed. There is wondrous light in this community of yours [Los Angeles] that is made of rock, of denseness - that which is called concrete jungle. There is illumination everywhere, within every cell of every beingness that is a particle of life. What is concrete in nature, it also is life. It also expresses sexuality, hm? This is a new concept here. You would consider it amusing to observe the mating habits, as it were, of such that you would consider to be inanimate. This is a time of much illusion about sexuality, of much consternation, pain, heartache, heartbreak and frustration; all of which is brought forward through the misunderstanding of Self, for you are operating in denseness, in physicality, experiencing a three dimensional reality of polarities expressed in maleness and femaleness.

God contemplated itself and created creation, that which you know of as life, in planetary form, in animal form, life breathing into itself the Isness called maleness and femaleness. It seeks to merge with itself through the polarities of opposites, of the genders known as male and female.

Your history, your culture and the humanity of eons past has sought to separate spirituality from sexuality, to separate God essence divinity within SELF from the physical Self called sexuality. This cutting off, or separating it from SELF - it is not contemplated that Self seeks to merge with SELF through merging the polarities. Therefore, through the cutting off, through some vows of chastity, the divine SELF is represented without expression in physicality through sexuality - therefore it is incomplete.

There is nothing wrong with it - but it is lacking wholeness. It is creating a void. That is why many of you feel an emptiness, for you are searching for the other part of SELF that can only be discovered in the other gender; through the merging of it, not only physically, but emotionally, mentally - soul essence merging. Through this merging, you unify the Source, the God essence within you. You merge into the totality that is issued forth through your embodiment.

Now, there is much to be said about masculinity and femininity in your society. Through the eons of time, what is masculine in nature has become powerful on this plane, but not as powerful as femininity. We shall explain this. You already know all of which I speak. I am merely your mirror reflecting your knowingness back unto you.

Now, eons ago in your time, it was accepted by both male and female that the purpose for the female was to please the sovereign essence, the male. That was accepted by both and allowed as reality, as it was created in those days. Therefore, the female, for her sustenance and life support, sought to please the sovereign, to please the leader of the harem. The value that was given to femininity was based only on age, beauty, and sexual prowess. The true value of the God essence within her was ignored. These are the value systems that have been carried forward even unto this day in your time. You are carrying soul essence memory, not only of your past, but of the opposite gender's past as well, for it is all part of mass consciousness, and being collectively of mass consciousness, you all participate in it. You all are a part of it. It is you, in exemplification of the whole; microcosmic within you - macrocosmic in society.

This value system has created fear in the female because you are not valued for your divine essence, but for that which is superficial in nature. Femininity indeed, is of darkness. Do you know why? It is not understood. The feminine mystique has always been mysterious, of darkness. What is darkness? Not being in the light. What is light? It is conscious understanding. The womb is a place of darkness, and darkness has as much validity in the Source, in God the Father, as does the light. They are merely different reflections of one another.

What is of the light is considered to be powerful, but darkness, that which is of feminine nature, is the ability to reach into that which is not perceivable and heal a child, or make predictions - this is femininity. It is not necessarily of female, but it is femininity. Each one of you carries within you both masculinity and femininity. Each one of you do, regardless of how your gender represents itself physically.

That has been feared by the male for eons, this mystique that he could not understand with his logical mind, therefore he sought to dominate, suppress and persecute the female so that he felt more powerful. This led to a crucial imbalance in the perception of male and female as equal genders. And believe me, all this of which I speak does relate to sexuality, because it relates to how you have relationships with one another, and how you interact with one another on a sexual level as well. As we unfold this further and further, for you to partake of the knowingness that abides within each and every one of you, you will also partake of the knowingness of your sexuality. Your spirituality (that which is God essence exemplified within you) and your sexuality (that which is God essence exemplified through physicality) is really one and the same. You have sought to separate them, and so you are separating physical interaction with another; that which is divine representation of the Source. You are cutting it off and separating it, considering it un-divine. There has always been this small voice saying unto you, as you participate in sexual relations, 'this is not divine, this is not godly'.

Therefore, for eons you have sought to suppress your sexuality for spirituality, forsaking one for the other, or so you perceived it to be, when really they were both divine manifestations of the God SELF. There is nothing wrong with expressing your gender through physical merging - expressing your gender of knowingness, not only your physical body, but your knowingness. The masculine is sovereignty, the crown upon your soul. Femininity is humility and unconditional love, the heart within the breast of your soul and together they make one whole soul essence. The merging of the two, this urgency within your being, throughout all of the eons of time, *this urgency to have a sexual relationship between man and woman, has been the urgency of the soul to merge the two parts of SELF.* That is why the loins have passion within them. The soul is desirous of re-expressing over and over again what it is to merge with SELF, to allow you to know the ecstasy on a physical level, so that you may know a much grander ecstasy on a soul level.

Another thing that has not been contemplated in your society is the void, the darkness, the deep, mysterious place of new life, new birth, called the womb, called female essence. This itself is the nature of the physical body, even if it is male. The nature of it is female. Let me explain this to you. The physical embodiment is made up of atoms - atoms, electrums, positrons - and there is much more space than density. The very nature of the physical embodiment expresses more void than matter. It is a receptacle. It is receptive. The physical embodiment is searching fervently, eon after eon, to merge with the soul essence. It is receptive to the grander essence that is known as you, that is also known as God. That is why you have this burning desire to become. Your embodiment and that which is your essence represented upon this Earth plane, is a fragment of your entire essence, it is receptive in nature. It is the birthplace of the new life called God exemplified. Your entire receptacle or temple, called your body, male or female, is feminine in nature. The planet is feminine; the sun is masculine, and they have a sexual relationship with one another.

That which is male upon this Earth plane is experiencing a thing that females have been experiencing for eons of time, and this is called change. It is traditional according to your society for the female to leave her family and go with the man of her choice, to change her circumstance, to change her name, and if there is dire circumstance or crisis, to change her outward circumstance to accommodate the male. Now males are learning change. They are becoming soft, compassionate, loving, more contemplative, less judgmental. They are not embodying all of this now, but this is the unfoldment that you are experiencing upon the Earth plane.

Do you know why there is so much change now, not only in mass consciousness, but with the male and the sexuality that is represented through male gender? It is because Mother Earth herself is changing, unfolding and bringing forth new life and new light into her planet called Terra. Change is represented in every focus of energy upon this planet, including sexuality. Those who have traditionally fit into a mould, have been accepted in what you call history and allowed to be. Those who do not fit into the mould are the ones that are involved and are experiencing the merging and unification of their maleness and femaleness. That is why they do not fit into the preconceived mould, and yet they are cut off from society and judged as less than divine, because they in truth are divine and are experiencing their divinity.

There is fear, fear of pain and fear of coming into your sexual relationship because of hurt, and because of previous experiences. You do not desire to be spat upon again. You see, vulnerability is no more than humility without the balance of sovereignty. There is nothing wrong with it. It is merely not balanced. That is why you feel so vulnerable. You have not experienced your sovereignty yet. You have not known it here yet. For if you truly are sovereign, there is nothing to fear at all, about anything. If you truly are sovereign, you are aware of your power in the seat of your being that is coupled with your heart seal. It is being realized that in sexuality, more and more heart connection is necessary to merge in harmony. Harmonious merging of the Source is allowing the heart connection, the unconditional love from both, and therefore, the penetration and allowance of the Source through both. It is a channel that is allowed to be, rather than being dammed up. What is feared is feminine essence. It is the void that is feared, and therefore, as it is feared more and more, it is allowed less and less in your experience of life circumstance. Therefore, you cut yourself off from expressing physically that which you are.

Merging is divine. It is also divine if experienced disharmoniously, for there is no judgment from the Source, or the God essence.

However, you would find it more fruitful, shall we say, if you allow it with the heart connection, because when you merge, you not only merge physically, you merge with your soul, you merge with the emotional body and its energies. It is an intermingling of energies, and what you take with you is not only passion released, but you take with you the soul essence memory of the person with whom you merged, because there is this intermingling. *That is why you can have this diseasement that is grand upon your plane now, even if the entity that you merged with did not have it resident within their cells, they had it resident within their soul memory, because they had intermingled with someone else that had it resident within their soul memory.* So you will find it very harmonious and fruitful to merge with those with whom you have a heart seal connection.

To express your gender physically and to have a sexual relationship, indeed, this is divine. Soul and body are one! That which is divine and that which is physical are one - not separate! Sexuality is divine essence. The heart and core of it is that you are merging with yourself, and therefore the Source is merging with itself. Pain will be no more when you are in true alignment with the Source within your being, for you will have no fear, and you will have no frustration. Chastity also will be aligned into the becoming process known as physical union - intercourse and interaction with the element called God that is of the opposite polarity. As you do this, you will find the energies moving from your root and your loin to the area known as the solar plexus. Then you have a passion, not necessarily of the loin, but a passion of power, and of sovereignty. As you balance this and merge it in fellowship with the heart seal, you will have a passion for unconditional love, along with sovereignty, which is true God illustrated - aligned, balanced and in harmony. Then you will find it rising not only in nature, but in frequency, to the crown seal. When you do this, as you walk upon this Earth plane you will find yourself in a sexual relationship with every essence that is life. The dew upon the leaves, a sunrise, the purple hued mountains, the grains of sand, the rising waves of the ocean, as it surges and ebbs, it is all sexual in nature.

You have a sexual relationship with every facet of life. As realized God, you will have ecstasy in this merging called sexuality, with all these facets of life, fragments of SELF, fragments of God. You will have passionate love exemplified. Your being will be on fire as the torch of you ignites into divine burning and illumination. It is a torch that is not extinguished either, for as it continues, it becomes the burning of the Source itself, as it is no longer resident in the crown, but goes forward, and you merge with the Source, in what is now called ascension. Therefore, it becomes the urgency of the Source, and not of the personality. As you accommodate this rising in frequency from your loins all the way to your crown, you will go through much change, transition, adaptation, further unfoldment and further knowingness. You will find your life aligning. You will find your experience joyful. You will find your relationships to be harmonious. You will find your love exemplified in every essence that is around you. *You will find yourself, really and truly, being happy.* The joy which comes from this fountain of ecstatic communication with the opposite gender and through that, with your own gender - through the different polarities that are exemplified all over this plane - will bubble and effervesce the ecstatic fountain and you will become the ever-flowing stream called God. As you gaze into your mirror, you will know that you have a sexual relationship with yourself and that you have a sexual relationship with God.

What is God, hm? It is ever changing, ever moving, ever creating and producing. It is both the active producing essence called male, and the grand mysterious void called female. It is both. Being created in the likeness of God, you contain both, ever changing, ever creating, ever producing and being very much a mysterious void the conscious mind does not understand.

Why do you think you are so enigmatic, not only to others, but even unto yourself? You do not understand why it is that you have frustrations with your mate and your lover, hm? It is because you do not understand the nature of the sexuality of you and, through that, of the Source. One of the reasons that the male has always harboured resentment and exerted some amount of dominion over the female is because the sexual nature of the female has always been perceived as the more powerful. A woman may entertain a lover for as long as she chooses, can she not? Therefore, for the eons of time, males have brought forth their own sovereignty in seeking to bring females into submission, because they felt powerless. They did not realize the divinity of the sovereignty that they exemplified in and of their own gender - different in nature, but equally valid. The females themselves have agreed. It was mutual. Understand that it was because of this agreement that you are becoming familiar with what it is to be male and female. *Sexuality is the means of expressing and experiencing harmony and reunion.* You do this by first experiencing separation, because only through contrast may you know what reunion is.

Questions and answers.

I will allow forum for now. You may query if you like.

Q: Some books say we can create what we so desire, and all we have to do is concentrate and it will manifest. I have been trying that and I am not too sure about my success and I really have not been too pleased with my results. Illness is still a part of me, along with the lack of this female relationship, and I am about ready to stop trying; perhaps that is the secret. I guess I have spent too much time trying to make it happen.

There are several issues to address here. I do appreciate your contribution, my dearest brother. I shall address each one. Trying merely indicates that you doubt it, that you doubt results, else you would not try, because you would know it already exists, hm? The bringing forth of a female relationship, or male relationship for you females here, that would bring you happiness, will not occur unless you already have your happiness and alignment of joy. As manifestor, if you place your happiness and joy and your divine Isness of SELF outside yourself into another entity, then this would indicate lack of joy in the Isness that you are, and lack of knowingness of your sovereign divinity, for you are seeking to express the union with the Source with someone else than you - and truly my brother, it is of you. When you know this in the heart and not try and think and contemplate, and desire to manifest, but *know*, then it will be.

As you issue forth the divine thought and *know it is already so*, this will manifest the joy within your being, which will allow what you desire to manifest to come unto you. If you have frustration and fear and fetterment within your being, then there is misalignment and the manifestor capacity of God, which is you, will also be misaligned and will not come into fruition because you have doubt, and this doubt becomes apparent in your manifestation - you know that it will not be so, but if you know that it *is* so, not will be, but IS already, though it is simply not manifested physically as yet, then it will be.

Ailment and illness are expressions of the Alter Ego within your being to give you a reason to doubt your capacity for divinity, to give you a point to contemplate that perhaps you are not sovereign. Indeed it is divine in its essence because it allows you to prove unto yourself that you are sovereign, by allowing the alignment to occur and the illness to dissipate. You see, the understanding of God is at easement and allowance with Isness, with All-That-Is. *And as you are at ease with your life as it is, with apparently no changes, then the changes you desire will appear.* What you call diseasement is 'not being at easement'. This applies to your sexuality as well and the grand diseasement of your plane. You are not at easement with your gender, and your own sexual nature. The sexual nature is only polarity expressed through the Source and as you come into the joy of the moment, without a relationship and without physical union, then the harmonious illustration of your embodiment will occur. Be at peace. Know that you are God, you are love, you are exemplified divinity and everything about you reflects all that you are at Source level - all that you are at soul level. If the reflection reflects unto you disharmony, discord and unhappiness, this is exactly your not becoming aware that God is within you. God is not unhappy. God is not disharmonious or discordant with life's circumstances.

Know indeed that you are divine expression, and that you are both genders. Your body may be one, but you are truly both, and all will heal itself. Healing is merely love energy allowing no division or misalignment. Love unconditionally All-That-Is, *as* it is.

Q: St. Germain, are you for or against monogamous relationships?

Neither, as either one is a judgment. When you are for something it is judgment as well, because it implies that you are against something else, alright? Monogamy is also a bondage or limitation, because it is expectation. You need not have a monogamous relationship with another entity. As long as you have a monogamous relationship with yourself, however, this is how it will result. Promiscuity will only lead to further frustration of a god, because the search for this union that will allow the knowingness of what polarity is, is not making the heart connection. It is superficial and thus the partners are becoming unfulfilled. This is what your sexual revolution two decades ago or so, brought into being - socially accepted promiscuity, but very unfulfilled beings - because they were not finding the seat of their power in sovereign union. Perhaps you will have no relationship physically upon this Earth plane. There is nothing wrong with that, for you need not experience it outwardly, because you have already experienced and captured the knowingness within your breast. Many entities do seek to participate in physical merging and union, because they are seeking what it means to be God expressed in the opposite gender, in a polarity situation, receptor and penetrator. You see, that is what the sun and Earth have in common. The sun is penetrator and the Earth is receptor, and there is a very heavy sexual relationship with both.

Change, indeed, occurs on the Earth as her seasons. The feminine in physical humanity also has her seasons, and the seasons are brought forth as the springing forth of new life. Spring indeed is the rebirthing period, and it occurs over and over and over again, and does not cease. It is limited man that has allowed the ceasing of this productivity of the female. The ceasing of the period in a female, a process you have called the end of the child-bearing age, need not occur. It is limited concentrated mass consciousness and denseness. This season not only occurs with woman and with Earth, but also occurs with the male and the sun, although it is less apparent. All is always changing, for the nature of physicality is femininity. That is the nature of your embodiment and that is the nature of your soul essence, receptivity - receptive to the capturing of the wisdom within circumstances - ever-seeking.

You see, you live in a masculine society that desires to have all the spaces filled. That is what masculine urgency is - to fill a space. It does not give validity to the fact that you can fill a space with emptiness, darkness, mystery, femininity, beauty and life born. You can fill this space to capacity with emptiness. It is a paradox, both full and empty, both essence, and non-essence. That is the very nature of polarities, of genders, and of sexuality.

Q: Why do relationships change? If one is close sexually with someone, and then it changes and there is divorce, or separation, why does that occur?

For one thing, because you choose it, and for another thing because life is constant change and as you surround yourself with life's circumstances, you respond to different circumstances for further unfoldment. You move in the flow of life and around the bends, as it were. Therefore, you will find yourself in circumstances allowing you to know what it is to change, because you cannot capture wisdom without contrast. It is within the experience of all of you to know what it is to be the perpetrator and perpetratee. So as you experience separation, view it not, and perceive it not truly as separation. View it as a circumstance that allows you union with the Source, because it allows you to know that you truly are God manifesting circumstances about you according to your own unfoldment, according to your own change. Your life will change and only a God can perform a miracle such as this.

Q: I feel you have been talking about Oneness at the level of the soul and I wonder if the only time on the physical level that one ever really is one, masculine and feminine, is in the act of intercourse?

But you see, intercourse need not be physical.

Q: Well, let us talk about physical intercourse for a minute.

Alright - popular subject upon this plane. Physical intercourse is merely interaction with penetration and reception. It is allowing you the ecstatic explosion called union completed. The spewing forth is fluid. The fluidity of knowingness spewing forth in the completion of the polarities known as male and female symbolizes the ushering forth of God. Everything in physicality has symbolic representation and meaning in the spiritual or soul essence or God understanding. Everything that you would consider spiritual, or God essence, is also represented symbolically in physicality. That is what is meant by 'as above, so below'.

What is sought after through physical intercourse by an entity within an embodiment is knowledge of itself. *God seeks to know itself through the union of the polarities.* However, it has been misunderstood through the eons and given meaning that was not intended to be. It has become third density. It has become superficial, and this is alright. It gives you contrast. It is divine. The rampant diseasement upon your plane allows you to know your choices, your options. Promiscuity is one, and the fervent desire to seek out that which is yourself. Love has been the reasoning behind much of this promiscuous merging. Seeking a love partner, only to be abandoned - what does this mean? You are seeking love, but you cannot have love from outside yourself until you have love within your own breast, for yourself. That is why you are feeling abandoned, for you have abandoned yourself, and it is represented as manifested reality outside yourself. You have the option of promiscuity. You have the option of monogamous relationships, and you have the option, my dearest brothers and sisters, of union without physicality. There is nothing wrong with this, but *the most harmonious experience upon this Earth plane, as God man, is to unite in physicality with another representation of your own soul essence, that which many have called soulmate.*

As you come into super-consciousness, you will indeed experience this, for merging at that point in your unfoldment and the Earth plane's unfoldment, will only be with soulmate; you are unfolded to the point where you will draw your soulmate unto you, magnetically, electromagnetically. It is a calling and they will respond and come unto you. That which abides as non-physical essence that is your soulmate will embody so that you may have completion and union. This may be in only an instant, for it will embody, perhaps, if you choose it to, at the moment of ascension. It need not tarry for long to have an ecstatic explosion of union as reality perceived upon this plane.

Femininity is intuition, knowingness without explanation, and what has been called healing as love. This is femininity. It is not necessarily of female body, but it is femininity. Much of the fear of this is also because eons ago, man and woman together collaborated in the choice to bring forth new life with pain and with imminent ceasing of the embodiment. Many of you have soul memory of the ceasing of your embodiment through bearing new life, and what is it that you are seeking now? The new life of you, birthing a new you. That is why so many of you are fearful. There is an urgency within you. You are fervent, but you are timorous. That is why you cling and hesitate. That is why so many of you, even though you meditate, contemplate and cogitate, have not come into the unfoldment and fruition of yourselves. It is because there is a soul level fear. It is not conscious, but a memory. Align this memory with the knowing that it was for a divine purpose, to bring forth ceasing of embodiment, and what is perceived as pain in order to introduce new life, allowing an essence to know what it was to experience femininity in that manner. Align it to the sovereignty and divinity it represents and you will not be so fearful of the birthing of the new you in harmonious circumstance, in peace.

Frustrated activity breeds frustrated activity. Frustration within sexual appeasement only breeds more, for you are in lack of light, in darkness if you will, of that which is of you - which is both polarities, positive and negative. I speak not only of genders, male and female, but I speak of organized creativity and of intuition. They are both apparent within every entity and, when you recognize that, you will no longer be frustrated, for you will realize the spectrum of you - all frequencies splayed before your very eyes, and that it *is* you. Each frequency of the light *is* you. You are prismatic, but you are only seeing, perceiving and knowing one or two of the hues which are represented by you. One of the hues which is perceived is your gender, which is manifested in physical form.

Male gender is understood as being the most superior, but this is not the case. They are both superior. There is nothing wrong with maleness. It is truly exquisite, beauteous beyond the comprehension of the males upon this plane, but there is also exquisite beauty in darkness, in what is womb-like, of which the conscious mind is not aware. If a thing is in the back of your mind, it is feminine, for it is not concretely apparent. It is in the dark - it is veiled. Anything that is not outwardly organized and perceived in a concrete and tangible fashion is femininity. Therefore, all your religions and spiritual dogmas through the eons are feminine, although they have perceived themselves as masculine. This is where the chaos comes into play.

In the 15th century, there was an organized understanding coming into play that called itself of the light. It was known as the Catholic Church. It sought fervently to stamp out the darkness and it began by severing the Jews and the dark people. Then it attacked the feminine mystique - not woman, but the mystique. Why is it that they were hiding and concealing the feminine mystique with their garb? The feminine mystique was known then as the craft. It was perception without tangibility, therefore they stamped out all that was not of the light, that was not of the dominating masculine power. That is why they were predominantly masculine in their organization. Have you ever heard of a female pope or cardinal, for that matter? As it continued in the 17th century, they began with the Inquisition, the crosses, incinerations and persecutions to stamp out darkness, which was femininity - the mysterious that was threatening to them, because they understood it not. You know, when the male essence understands it not, it finds it threatening. So this continued until you have what you have today in your time, which is a misunderstanding and disharmony between the religious understandings in Christianity or spirituality, a misunderstanding of the sexual dramatization of God essence. All are participating individually in the drama of mass consciousness, through sexual relationships.

Now it is time to come into a knowingness of what this drama has given you. This inquisition, all of this persecution, it has given you much. It is blessed because it has given you the knowing of what this experience is, what it is to be persecuted for being female, what it is to be confused because you are male, what it is to be confused because you are female and you are persecuted and you feel you have done nothing wrong. Eons ago if an entity was born female, they were cast away. Many of them were put on piles and devoured by vultures, because they were not sovereign. Their souls had no value in those times, but it has all been for the purpose of divine knowingness, and to bring forth experience - all of it is blessed! There is no judgment upon it, but you may capture the bread basket that has been given unto you through experience. Partake of it. Feed yourself with it. When you do this, you will become aligned and harmonized with both polarities. As you realize your sovereignty, you will have no dissension between male and female in your sexual expression, for it will be realized as sovereign and divine.

The judgment of your embodiments - do you know that only females are really that judgmental of their embodiments? Most of you males have no concern about it. It is because the females have been so judged and persecuted if they were not of the beauty, the age and sexual prowess that was desired. Therefore, as you come into the knowingness that even you females are male - which is sovereign, which is light, which is kingdom realized, manifestor, creator, beauty bringing forth light - you are the sun [son] in both spellings. As you become male in your knowingness, you will become neither, for you will be both. As this occurs with each one of you, including you males - as you capture within your being the softness, compassion, the intuition, the love, the void that is called darkness, which is not understood - as you become veiled and appreciate the mystery and awe of life, you also will allow yourself to be both male and female, without judgment of yourselves based on social consciousness. As you capture both, you will be God itself exemplified, for God is also neither. You will also have less concern about physicality. You will not put so much emphasis on your appearance. As you release into the Source and give up into the All-That-Is, called God the Father (that is what you call it and it is not a male), as you give up your consternation about your physical appearance, lo and behold, you become manifestor. Then you can manifest your embodiment in whatever way you choose. You may manifest and create for yourself the beauteous embodiment you so desire, but only once you release its importance.

The female has always been so concerned about appearance, because in the past, eons ago, this is how she attracted her support. This is how she received her life. Substance was only given unto her, if she was beauteous, youthful, sexual and sensuous and all of these things. Otherwise she was cast upon the heap with all the rest of the worthless items. That is why there is such emphasis upon it in your culture now. It need not be so and, as you come into the merging of the knowingness, the male of the female within, and the female of the male within, all of this will dissipate and there will only be peace, harmony and love abiding. You need not be so concerned about whether you are sexually appealing or not, both male and female. Males will not have to conceal their bald spots and the women do not have to conceal their over-abundant spots. You will rejoice in your Isness.

Q: Could you elaborate on the sexual relationship we have with the sun and Mother Earth?

The desire of entities to go and bask in the sun, is basking in the light, basking in the power, in the creative energy expressed in an organized understanding called light rays. Mother Earth - you have a sexual relationship with her as well. When you desire support, you go hence into Mother Earth, to nurture yourself of her water, the ocean, her flora; to walk upon the ground unshod and to run unfettered through fields. This is freedom. This is nurturing and support. The depths of darkness are of the ocean, the darkness of the soil upon the land and the depth of the caverns. Cavern - that is a feminine symbol in nature. The rivers flowing - she has her seasons. You embrace it all, for it affects all of you, and how it affects you is what I mean by sexual relationships. You feel supported by Earth. You feel empowered by the sun - solar energy - power. You see, the water also has power too. It is not given the credit and validity as equal unto the sovereign sun.

There were many entities in the cultures of the past - Egyptian, South American, etcetera, who worshipped the sun. They have also worshipped Jehovah [masculine energy, Alter Ego personified] and they have also worshipped the essence that is God - the creative force - as male. God is not male. They have called it God, the Father, because they have given it the characteristics and assigned it the beingness that is sovereign and powerful, and at times rending without the balance and harmony of unconditional love, without the sustenance, the support, the mystery. If there is anything that is mysterious, it is God, which also indicates that God is of female essence as well as male. The rain upon your plane; it is female, pouring forth from the sky. It induces calm. This is why it is so rhythmic, why it lulls you into slumber, because it is nurturing, it heals and it produces abundance in your fields, but so does your sun in the sovereign shining forth of its rays. They are both valid and wondrous and awe-inspiring, and both are in a sexual relationship, because sexuality is no more than the understanding of polarities.

Q: St. Germain, having a sexual experience with all that exists is making love with all that exists, experiencing the ecstasy and creating beauty?

Indeed, and you are re-establishing its validity within your own being. Thank you, my dear.

Q: St. Germain, homosexuality and bisexuality have been in existence throughout time. I think it was more accepted back in what we call history. Why has today's society become so judgmental?

It is not judged more now than it was then. It has always been judged, for it has been considered and perceived to have been unnatural, but everything that exists is natural, or it would not exist. Merging with your own gender is merely expressing fear of the opposite gender, for its myriad reasons. The merging of male with male is seeking of the void, without experiencing the fear represented by the actual female. That which is female with female is experiencing passion for the sensitivity and passion for the mutual giving, not only of sensual pleasure, but of emotional sustenance, without risking countenance with the male represented in physicality.

You see, the life preservation instinct in all of humanity is so intense that it allows the pathway of the least risk. Openness was always considered to be risky, for much pain had been encountered, much frustration and utter desolation, because of openness in many relationships of the past. So 'why shall I open myself again', you say unto yourselves, 'to be hurt yet again?'. You would consider it risky. You are becoming the void when you open your heart seal to allow mutual exchange - which is called intercourse - not only of physicality, but intercourse of all other manner as well. Seeking to merge with the void, is seeking to merge with the void called the Source, but in a microcosmic understanding - upon this Earth plane in physical relationships. Therefore, you close yourself and separate yourself from yourself, and as you do this, you are no longer receptive. Therefore, you seek relationships without risk, without perceived risk. Many times you turn unto your own gender, because you know what your own gender is like. It is considered safe. That is why an entity would do this. Why they are judged is because it is not known *why* they do this. It is of the darkness and is considered unnatural. It is not the accepted practice, the known activity. Therefore, it is considered to be of the darkness. Everything of the darkness is feminine in nature and has always been judged, because of the nature of this plane and because of the nature of separation.

When God contemplated SELF and decided to create the experience of polarity, femininity - that which is not outwardly apparent - has been persecuted as a result of this and placed upon the altar of sacrifice for eons. That is why the scientific community constantly refuses and rejects everything that is not readily and visibly apparent, including that which is extra-terrestrial, including extra-sensory perception and all the senses that are not physical, because it is unknown, of the darkness and therefore feminine. It is very powerful, and that is another reason it is feared, because the results of this power can be felt and sensed, but not understood with an organized understanding.

So, the male essence of Alter Ego perceives fear and this is alright. There is no judgment. Allow yourself to feel the fear, acknowledge it, embrace it, love it and let it be as it is. Go forth in your new knowingness that this fear is a part of you, join hands with it, embrace it and go onward in a unified knowing. Do not judge yourself - any part of yourself - your maleness, your femaleness, how you express your sexuality, or what your relationships are. Do not judge yourself, for in judging yourself, you are judging the Source within your being and you are separating yourself from yourself.

The exchange of fluids through a physical union is exchanging that which is fluid in nature of the Source, on-going Isness, constant motion, fluidity, going with the flow. So rejoice when you exchange your fluids. Rejoice when you exchange the love of all of life, in a sexual manner. Rejoice when you embellish another with pleasure, for you are also embellishing the mirror of you with pleasure. You are becoming God exemplified, for you are knowing joy in harmonized union.

Go forth, I say unto you now, and have a sexual experience with everything you have countenance with - everything - your mate, your siblings, your parents, the sun, the Moon, the Earth, the feathered friends of yours that warble in the trees in the night, the flora, and all that is perceived as inanimate. Spirituality is God essence. Sexuality is God essence expressing in physicality. They are both one. There is no difference. They are merely different facets of exploration and knowingness through this exploration.

So, go forth into this journey, this voyage and this adventure called sexual relationship. Explore the divinity of maleness and femaleness, understand and know the polarity of All-That-Is. Go forth with joy in your hearts. Partake of the sexual with a different knowingness, with a different meaning. Partake of merging in a different manner. Ignite the spark of life called passion, for all of life. So be it.

I will bid you farewell for now.

Indeed, it is truly my honour to be in your presence, and I partake heartily of expressing my own sexuality when I come into an awareness such as this. As I reflect upon all the mirrors here, the divine illustration of sexuality is apparent within all of you, and is mirrored back unto that which be I. The different fragments of what is considered to be I, and facets, is expressed by all of you and I love you heartily for this illustration, and I partake joyously. Partake of yourselves in like manner.

Namaste.

Chapter 4

ECSTATIC EXPLOSION

Greetings, my beloved brothers and sisters. It is wondrous to be with you this evening of your time. Your energy, the intertwining of your essence is creating a grand pool of love, brotherhood and communion, and the light of the universe is indeed abiding herein.

So we come here this evening to understand what be orgasm, hm? That does conjure up some interesting visions. It is the creation of the divine life force into the extension of the God I Am essence. The understanding of orgasm is the flow of the divine life force into the cosmos and into the essence of creative force - the essence of that which creates life upon the plane, indeed of the unseen and of the seen, the physical and the non-physical. All are created of the divine life force. Indeed, the merging in physicality, the sexual experience, is divinity coming forth to experience itself with another; two divine entities desiring to come together to become One through union in physicality. It is the desire of the soul essence for Oneness, the unity of the God I Am, to create communion, the balance - the harmony of the polarities - which are abiding as male and female. Gender is indeed only the opposite polarity of the sameness. It is you. It is merely a different polarity.

Now, electricity has a positive and a negative charge. However, there is not a flow of electricity until the two are joined and in the merging of the balanced polarities in harmony, there is a flow. There is an orgasm of sorts - a surge of energy into the light, into the explosion that you understand as illumination. That is what occurs when the two essences of polarity come together in physicality to cause an explosion of orgasmic understanding.

The essence that be I was once, in your understanding of a previous lifetime, in what you call a tavern, and I saw an entity of female nature who experienced life through her hair. Indeed, she identified herself with her hair. That is the only understanding she had of beauty, and she brought it forth into the experience of all the other entities as well, in splendid display and array of her crowning glory, so that she could be understood as divine. There was another entity who was of male essence that understood his identity through an interesting display of ink upon the skin - that which you call a tattoo. It was live art - a dragon tail that never stopped, indeed. This was his understanding of his identity as divine. He displayed it for all to see, quite boastfully indeed. But nothing is accidental. Have you ever bumped into a tattoo needle by accident?

All things are for a purpose. All experiences are brought forth for the creation of knowingness. Therefore, the identity these entities sought in that which was without is exactly the same as with other entities who are in constant search for physical gratification outward of themselves, that is seeking soul essence fulfilment in the embodiment, in superficial physical passion. They will never come into their knowingness, for gratification and fulfilment of the soul essence is not outward of you, it is inward of you. Those entities that are understood as being promiscuous are saying unto the Earth plane, unto the whole of life: 'Fill me, fill me, fill me!' They are constantly in search of fulfilment, but they never find it, because the fulfilling comes from the knowingness of the God I Am within you, not without you.

When you fill the chalice from the cup of the Christus within, that is the crucible of the eternal essence, that indeed is the fluid, the river, as it were, of the soul within your being coming forth, you ignite the passions of life, and the joy therein, and explode in an ecstatic understanding of the God I Am of all of life - divinity expressed in the whole of life. That is the ecstatic explosion! Some have called it ascension. Some call it 'going forth into the void of the forever'.

When you understand the beauty of life - the silvery leaf in the spring rain, tossed about laughingly, revealing its underside flirtatiously to the breezes that come to caress it - that is experiencing joy. Bringing forth and cherishing within your heart the beauty of the sublime intertwining of the tendrils of the vine, of the golden tresses of a youth as they clutch one another in the playful contemplation of the breezes. That is the essence of the joy of life and bringing it forth into your heart and circulating it to the silence of the polarities and spewing it forth into the universe - *that* is ecstatic explosion! That is passion! That is orgasm.

The superficial understanding through physicality is a manner of experiencing orgasm, but it is not fulfilling and it will indeed continue the search. You will forever be upon the pathway of 'fill me, fill me, fill me.' You will forever have lovers in your bed who do not allow you to perceive your own divinity, for you do not understand that they are mirrors. You do not understand that the divinity, the God and the fulfilment is *yourself*, the origination point, the Source of it. As you experience life upon this plane, you will encounter many other entities. All of them are the Christus. All of them are your lovers! All of them, indeed, even the ant upon the ground as it carries upon its back the nutrition for the next few hours, even that is your lover. You become the lover of life.

The love-life of the modern monk is indeed the mating of the Christus, bringing forth the beauty and splendour of divine love within his breast. It is the penetration of the veil that is drawn upon the consciousness of the plane. This veil prevents the perception of the explosion of the flow of life to come into you and out through you and exchange with you in a knowingness that creates abundance. It indeed expounds your experience of yourself, of your soul essence.

Sexual energy on this plane is the Source energy. It IS the essence of life. As you experience it in the exchange of your fluids and intermingle them with one another, indeed, as you exchange your embraces with one another, you will exchange the knowingness of one another, for your soul essence is intertwined and embraced as well, not only your physical embodiment. Doing this, you partake of the knowingness of the other entity and bring forth the essence of their experience into your own being, and you indeed expand your awareness in this manner. Acknowledge that your physical union is a divine aspect of God I Am. There is nothing wrong with it. It is wondrous to express love to another entity in this manner, in a manner that is indeed powerful and potent; in a manner that no other expression upon this plane can be. It allows you to understand passion of third density so that you may understand the passion play of God, which is the creation of the universe.

A star is born because of the ecstatic explosion of a God. It is the ejaculation of light into the universe, the flow of divinity piercing and penetrating the etheric planes to bring forth the life of a star to be perceived by all those who abide in its presence, in splendour and magnificence. Indeed, it is a golden jewel brought forth as the essence of life for the understanding of its beauty. That is why you experience passion, that you may understand what it is that you bring forth. You may understand what it is to balance and repolarize your energies so that you may understand the beauty and divinity of those with whom you exchange it. As you embrace, you embrace not only an entity, you embrace humanity. It is a microcosmic expression of the embrace of the whole of humanity.

As you spew forth your love, as you spew forth into the depths of you, you relish your understanding of life and the pleasure within it. You spew that forth into the universe, indeed, into the cosmos of excitability within you, the joy, and it ignites the flame of passion within you. It is the burning, the desire to merge with all of life into the whole of life to become unified and powerful, to become God I Am. That is what the urge, the search to merge, is. It is the desire to know God, to know God through that which is outward of you so that you may complete your awareness of this plane.

All entities, both male and female, contain positive and negative. When the two merge, your positive and negative energies balance. Both of them do, and you may bring forth the surging within your genitals and allow the exchange to occur with your pituitary gland, which is the hormonal balancer of your systems. It allows the access, the fluid to flow through you to open, to flower, to blossom, to understand the power to be the receptacle of it and to bring forth penetration of your universe to create miracles.

The blossoming of a flower - do you know what it is? It is the beauteous splendour of a bud penetrating the air to allow receptivity of the power and love of the universe. It is the essence of the homogenization of the genders. It is both male and female in this manner, as all of you are. It is balancing and allowing the beauty to be understood. So this passion play that you call your life, it is indeed a passion play. Depending on how you choose your teams, as it were, you determine what your experience will be - the teams of your male and female energy, and how you allow the game to progress. It is a game of life - truly it is. Your embraces are at times preceded by what you call a kiss, hm? A contraction of the lips due to an enlargement of the heart. But you know, that which is a kiss is merely the tender caressing of another entity in acknowledgment of their divinity. You may kiss their cheeks, their tears, their hair, their hands, but the most divine response that you can bring forth within another entity is when you kiss their soul. You can kiss it tenderly with your own by bringing forth the Christus within them, by acknowledging the beauty and divinity within them.

Promiscuity is rampant upon the land in your now. It experiences a bit of a curbing - not quite as much touch and go. It is alright. What you understand as promiscuity is only the fervent search that will align itself, that will reharmonize when allowed to run its course. It has been the case for eons. Promiscuity is not what you call a modern invention. It has been rampant upon this plane for eons of time and it will rebalance in the time of super-consciousness, because it cannot help but understand that what is sought is within. It is indeed an ancient teaching that will come into a realization. Know thyself. Know the truth and the truth shall set you free.

Many of you do not have a lover, a sexual partner who you may bring to your bed, as it were. For many, this is nothing to sneeze at, but I will tell you, in truth it is really not important that you exchange physically with a partner. That is wondrous and divine in its own right, but it is not something which has to be! It is not a necessity. The necessity is to recognize the whole of life as your lover. Your whole essence will be merged with the essence of the God I Am of the universe. That is what will merge you with the grand void.

The creation of the ecstatic explosion into the joy of ascension will allow you to revere God and the divine essence within all of life - and your mates, your lovers, and indeed your siblings - all of humanity, and all of nature. They are all your lovers - all of them. Understand their beauty. Capture the rapture of the embrace within your heart through the awareness of the joy of it. Penetrate the veil. Be receptive and open, flower, as it were, and be the receptacle for this knowingness, as you penetrate yourself. Let the semen of the soul penetrate the grand and vast void of the universe. Become explosive. Become a supernova! Bless the universe with the juices of the soul. You know what the juice of the soul is? It is your tears. Sweet nectar of a flower that is in blossom. All of you are coming here this evening of your time to understand physical union, physical passion, the fruits of the labours of love. All you need do, my dearly beloved brethren, is gaze into the mirror and you know it all - and yet, you walk away from the mirror scratching your head. It is alright. I shall be here again to tell you, over and over again, until you get it.

I love you all so grandly. I give forth my essence unto you so that you may indeed reflect in this mirror to know that which you be, to know indeed that for which you search, to know indeed your lover. Discussing lovers seems to be quite a pastime upon this plane. It is only because you will eventually understand that you are the lovers experiencing yourself as separate from yourself, only to remerge with *yourself* in all aspects and come into the divine union, the wedding of God.

Indeed, burst forth in fullness. Allow yourself to be pulsating, weeping with wonderment at life, with love. Give forth your passion. Give it forth without discretion, without judgment. The passion of a hummingbird sitting on the ledge, gazing into your eyes, beating at a higher frequency to be sure, mirroring your own essence at a higher frequency, beating its breast with its wings - understand what it harbours within its heart. The love of the beauty within that tiny fine-feathered friend - that is passion - when you understand what it represents. Spewing forth your semen, in a physical manner, will indeed give you contentment for the moment, but you will also experience exhaustion of your essence energy, for you are not allowing the harmonious balance, the recirculating of the polarities and the understanding of the divine eternal fountain from whence it comes. That is why you feel so exhausted after expending much of this energy. You feel depressed, discontent, unsatisfied, because you are not replenishing yourself with your own fountain. You are turning on the spigot and allowing the drain to gobble up your essence. You do not understand what the Source is. You do not understand that you can turn it on again any time you wish, of your own essence, without the complement of another.

Your maleness and femaleness upon the plane and the merging thereof is not a power play for the supremacy of love. It is indeed the complement of one another in the divine union of supreme love. Maleness and femaleness are not only of your physical embodiment. Maleness and femaleness are not bodies. They are essences. The sun is male essence. The Earth is female essence. The moon is female essence. The spewing volcano is a male essence. The ocean of life is female.

You see, you can partake of the complementary nature of life in other manners than merely union with another physical embodiment. Watch yourself, bathe yourself in the wonderment of your own soul. You can do this when you immerse yourself within the spring of life, within the constant flowing of the divine essence upon the Earth. Nature is indeed a powerful mirror in this manner. The birds and the bees - that is where it came from. You explain unto your siblings what life is - through the example of nature - and I am telling you a different aspect about the birds and the bees now.

There are those of you that are male, who have never encountered a mate to take and wed, you call yourself bachelor. The females among you who have a yearning, a desire for completion, who have not found a mate for their bed, but find it empty and cold, all of you will become reharmonized and rebalanced. As you express joy in your daily life, going forth into the explosion of cosmic joy each moment, as you penetrate it with your experience, in each understanding of the now, it will fulfil this yearning, but first you must know the joy! It is the initial understanding *before* the completion of your wants and desires. For this divine thought energy, when placed into the universe, into the creative force called God I Am, will allow unmanifest energy to manifest as physical reality. That is what will allow you to experience your soulmate upon this plane. In super-consciousness, all will have a mate, for they shall call forth what you call soulmate and all shall merge in union with their soulmate. It shall be born of the divine love. The creative forces shall intermingle with one another and create the balance of polarities and harmonize the energies. Indeed, with this union, there shall be an ecstatic explosion of cosmic joy, ascension understood and beauty become aware.

The perception of the creative force within each and every entity shall bring this into manifestation. Only through this awareness can this occur, only when you perceive the beauty of the joy of each moment and not when you perceive loneliness and heartache and heartbreak, for that is merely the understanding to seek your happiness outward of you. Happiness is a choice of each moment, not a result. As you make this choice in every moment, the happiness bears forth the fruit of your desires, from the womb of your knowingness.

Impregnate yourself with joy and wonderment of life. You did not know that men could impregnate themselves, did you? But they can, for a body is not an essence, it is not a soul - it is merely the representation in physicality of a partiality of the soul. The completion of it, the experience of the eruption in the heat of passion - that is love divine. That is joy divine. That is God experienced! That is orgasm of the supreme kind.

Sexuality will take on a whole new meaning upon your plane before long in your time. It already is in transition. Quite a rampant one at that. Superficiality is being understood for what it is. Going beyond the obvious is becoming commonplace. Going into the soul essence, the heart and core of an essence, of a soul, that is becoming the understood reality - that is super-consciousness, heaven on Earth. Indeed, the merging of male and female is the key being placed into the lock opening the gates to the kingdom of heaven. Kingdom of heaven on Earth, indeed. It is the understanding of supreme and divine love on Earth, the passion of life being exhibited within every moment. It is the experience of ecstatic union and new life upon the plane in the joy, the glow, the resonance and radiance of God understood, of the beauty and splendour within every magnificent cell of your being. That is indeed the experience you shall know.

You know, when you come forth in divine resonance of God I Am within you, your embodiment begins to pulsate, your respiration increases, your system comes into a higher frequency, becomes accelerated, speeded up, as it were. Your heartbeat pounds, you enter a higher vibration and you glow, you become radiant. You become enlightened. As this harmony abides within you constantly, the constant emission of joy of your soul will be your non-ceasing experience of life as radiance. It will be your expression of eternity on this plane - your fountain of youth. Youth is the acknowledgment of the ever-present birthing of new life, where each cell of your body will be born yet again every moment as you re-experience cosmic joy.

When you emerge yourself in this passion, this merging of physicality in divine union, all your cells will explode, all of them will ejaculate. All of them will have an orgasm within their own being! All of them will ignite into the flame and the fire of burning desire - all of them. Would that not be wondrous? That ignition of the flame of the burning desire within you will be the transmutation, the alchemical understanding of physicality merging into the soul essence of the God I Am of the foreverness. That will bring the physical into the non-physical - you have called it ascension.

How do you think automatic combustion occurs? Automatic human combustion - that is what it is - passion brought forth into an explosion of every cell of your being, and it is initially understood through the orgasm of sexual embrace. The embrace of lovers beneath the moonlight laughingly harnessing one another's energies together, intermingling into supreme love - that will be merely one taste, one savouring of what shall occur upon the plane in super-consciousness. Go forth under the moonbeams and embrace her, embrace the essence of the silvery ball of light, which is the jewel of the heavens, the priceless pearl of the night. As you embrace her, you shall know passion, you shall know the understanding of fervent burning desire, yearning to penetrate the veil of life, to understand its mysteries, to bring forth awareness of the mystique of it. Penetrate it, and you shall understand explosive ecstasy, the joy of the reality of life understood. Indeed, go forth in this manner and experience, embrace the moon and all she becomes to you. Indeed, see children - your siblings, as laughter enlivening the world to understand what passion is! Passion is not going forth in the heat of the [sexual] drive. *Passion is joy.* Passion is fervent playfulness. That is what passion is. You will understand this when you understand your siblings as they play in the wilderness, as they play even at the hearth of your home. They exhibit passion about everything, regardless of how mundane it may seem to you, regardless of how insignificant or trivial it may appear, they are passionate about it. They are immersing their being into that moment of enjoyment. That is the joy of life. That will bring you into the perception of orgasm of all of life - when you understand this experience every moment of your life.

The next time you weep, next time you ejaculate, next time you perspire, next time you understand a tear upon the breast of your brethren, you will understand passion. That is passion, is orgasm in that moment. Indeed, you will come to know life as life is understood by God, as passion and orgasm! Quite a complement.

Questions and answers.

Q: What is the purpose of AIDS here on this Earth?

To be an aid to the Earth plane to understand superficiality and the perception of the beauty that is indeed beyond the surface of the skin. It allows the perception of the soul, with the soul, the understanding of the beauty within you, going beyond the obvious. It affords entities the opportunity to be particular, to be cognizant, to be aware of their choices. As this awareness blossoms unto them, they shall perceive the divinity within the diseasement, for they understood it as their teacher, and they shall bow unto it in reverence, for they shall know that they have been taught by the mirror of this grand diseasement. You see? Bless it, for it brings forth grand wisdom. It is not terminal. Nothing is impossible to God. Alright?

Q: What about the tantric understanding?

The tantric understanding is the preservation of your semen, of your fluids. There is some limitation within this. It is a divine teaching, but perceive it as limiting, for it tells you not to do a [certain] thing. There is nothing that is either/or in the understanding of God I Am. It is all *and*.

You see, you can enjoy the circulation of your fluids within your embodiment and the direct connection of plugging in, as it were, to the Source essence, the God I Am essence, *and* allow the fluid to go forth from you in harmonious balance of the energies. Not disharmonious. Harmonious, you see? You will find yourself in a whirlwind if it is discordant and disharmonious and not balancing. You will find yourself being lonely and desiring of an embrace, a yearning, but when it is a harmonious balance of energies, you will find yourself in the feeling and sensation of completion, fulfilment understood. In the Tantric understanding the preservation of this fluid is merely symbolic. Allowing your fluids to go forth into the rest of the rivers of life will complete the union of humanity. You see, there are thousands of rivers that go forth into the sea, and the sea is never filled and the rivers are never depleted. It is the same thing, my dear.

It is a constant source to the rivers and the rivers are a constant source to it.

Q: St. Germain, is mating understood in fourth density?

Indeed, of soulmates.

Q: I mean the sexual mating.

That is of which I speak. There is also birthing.

Q: I have experienced a few times a condition of the body being in almost a super-heat, but not heat so much in the physical sense, but almost like a sacred sort of feeling, like..

A divine fever. You know, divinity sneaks up on you when you least expect it. It is always the case. When you are in hot pursuit of it, it alludes you, and when you sit and contemplate the rest of the universe, it will alight on your arm, likened unto a butterfly. The divine fever, the experience of a heat that is not heat, is the rising of the vibration of the energies within you - a higher frequency, an acceleration. It is the perception of the conception of the universe and the birthing of it all in one moment. It is explosive in its experience, yet without temperature, but indeed with the understanding of a flame.

Q: Is that what is called kundalini rising?

That is only part of it. That is where it originates from. The sensation itself and the knowingness itself is the spontaneous result of this as it flows forth from the root, from the kundalini forth unto the crown, out into the universe - and yet back again into you. It is the circulation of your energy which balances the polarities. Experience in this manner is cosmic awareness. It is but a taste, but a sampling of what is possible when every moment is constant ecstasy.

I desire you to partake of this hotline of you, when you find yourself in frustration, when you find yourself in indigestion or in an isolated understanding. You know *ulcers are not a result of what you eat, but what is eating you.* When you find yourself in a misalignment of life, pick up your hotline. Indeed, allow it to spew into you, and as it pours into the deepest recesses of you, release the friction through the lubrication of the love of life. Love of life. Do not merely exist within life, letting life pass you by as you ignore it, *but love it!* Participate with it. Tap your energies in mutual exchange with it. That is loving life. Understand the nature of it, the wisdom and knowingness of it. Exchange your knowingness with one another, and you will feel completed, for you will have had a sort of orgasm with it, a balancing of energies, a harmonizing. As you do this with all of life, it will automatically spill over into the rest of your experience, including your mating procedures. You will find yourself abed, as it were, with a desire of your heart, and it need not be physical - I reiterate this. Perhaps it will be if your desire is fervent enough, the desire for love of life, not for the other mate, for that one will come in the ripeness of its time. The happiness within your heart will draw unto you, likened unto a magnet, that which is your soul essence desire. You become more electrified, more magnetic, more charismatic to that which is your heart's desire. If only you understood your power potential, you would plug in right now. Well - you shall.

Allow the wind to be your lover. Let it embrace you, massage you, caress you, whisper sweet nothings in your heart. Allow it to participate with you in the most intimate of moments, as you unveil and reveal yourself to it, from the depths of you. Penetrate it with your joy and it will carry it to the ends of the universe. Spill over effervescently with the bubbles of you, hm? Soda pop, divine soda pop. Doing this, you will bless everyone and everything you encounter. In this blessing comes forth ecstasy, explosive joy, cosmic awareness, divine union, one with another with another with another, until all the pieces of divinity are merged into the wholeness of God. Cradle yourself and all the rest of humanity within your embraces. Lick their wounds, as it were. Allow your love to spill all over them, for this is the love of humanity. This is the love of the Christus. This is the love of God.

Do you understand? I love you all so grandly. I give unto you the chalice of the God I Am, for you to intermingle with, for you to embrace, for you to also spill your fluids into so that they may become united and one and ignited with the flame of divine love.

,

I give my heart to you - I give my soul essence unto you. I give all I AM unto you, for you are my brethren. You are my others. You are the life of God that I have desired for the eons of time to come unto and merge with. I am here. Gaze unto this mirror and know that which be you. Know the love I give unto you. I lead you back unto the chalice of yourself. Drink of it heartily, and share it with the rest of the world. Go forth now and be passionately playful and playfully passionate. So be it.

Go forth now, my dearest beloveds, and be cosmically orgasmic - constantly explosive in ecstasy, and indeed you shall know joy. Farewell for now.

Namaste.

Chapter 5

THE FRUIT OF PASSION

A new galaxy here? Indeed illustrious stars, all of you. Luminous, twinkling of your own essence, beauteous beyond comprehension, contributing to the art of creation in the heavens. Indeed you are wondrous. It is truly my honour to be in your presence. We have come forth here this evening to understand the fruit of passion - the olive - which is understood to be aphrodisiac in nature, creating the passion, the fervent desire of your loin. Sounds exciting?

Do you understand why the olive is known as the fruit of passion? The olive was the initial fruit on this Earth plane. The olive is the combination of the elements that give what you call passion. And what is passion? Fervent desire. Indeed.

Passion is the essence of the life force within an entity or that which you understand as God. The Christ-consciousness that was born in the embodiment called Jeshua, Jesus, the heralder of the Piscean age, understood passion, and it was understood throughout the Piscean age and culminates in experiential awareness outwardly in what you call the Aquarian age. The passion that was experienced by Jeshua in the garden of Getsemane is symbolized by the continuance of the olive tree in that area and it will continue to grow and bear fruit ad infinitum, for eternity. It is the symbol of the passion of the Piscean age. What was experienced in the garden of Getsemane? All that you would understand as emotion - fear, bitterness, anger, love, joy, jealousy, greed, hunger, thirst - all the emotions. All of them were experienced with fervent desire indeed. The culmination of these emotions bring the awareness of Christ-consciousness - and that is to be understood as the vibration of ecstasy of God.

When it is perceived in an unlimited fashion, it is ecstasy. On this Earth it is has been understood as victory. That is why the leaves of the olives were placed as a crown upon the head of the Olympic Gods who were victorious during the Olympic games in ancient Greece. The olive branch is known as peace, why? Because it is the understanding of power and unconditional love in harmonic balance, creating sovereignty. Green is the colour of the olive. Green is the colour of the heart seal. It is love.

In your limited awareness of third density, passion is understood as sexual energy within the loin area. However, if you expand it into unlimitedness, the rising of the vibration from the loin area through to the crown will afford you the unlimited understanding of what passion is beyond third density. The obvious is third density. The unobvious is the unlimited known as fourth density and beyond. The obvious is sexual exchange. The unobvious is ecstatic energy exchanged with the universe. What is it that occurs during sexual exchange, hm? The energies are exchanged. The fluid of the male is thrusted unto the female, the woman, and the woman absorbs this energy, the negative and positive in union together.

You know, negative charge is not electricity and positive charge is not electricity, but the unified balance and flow of the two together - this is electricity. The unified balance and flow of your maleness and femaleness together in one entity as experienced in and of itself, this is *the* electricity. This is the ecstasy of orgasm in the cosmic sense. This is what is called passion. When you allow the flow without congestion, without resistance, you have a completed circuit. The female is very psychic. She has the lunar understanding indeed, and during this particular season of the female, there is much dispensation of energy - of life force. Therefore, as it is dispensed, it is in her nature to have the ultimate charge replenished within her essence to continue bringing forth more of this energy. That is why she has potential for sexual energy.

The thrusting forth of the fluid of the male essence, the ejaculation, is indeed passion exploding. The semen contains within it three to five hundred million sperm cells - enough to repopulate this your country. So it is also a grand powerful source of life force. Both are. The union, the combination of the male life force and the female life force in harmonic balance, creates joy beyond unlimited comprehension. God is this balance - God exemplified through passion is this balance.

Your query is about moving the vibration of the passion from the lower seals into the area of your solar plexus and crown. This is your quiz unto yourself. How does one do this? You frustrate yourselves and have much consternation about this. 'Shall I become celibate?' you say unto yourselves. 'Shall I force myself to inhibit my own flow of energy that is quite natural unto any entity? What shall I do to allow the continuance of the energy without inhibition, without congestion of the seals and still raise the energy upward?'

The key here is to change the course of the energy into a circular motion, rather than simply releasing it. Circulate it. Imagine your spine as a hollow straw, drawing forth the energy from your loin, your root area. Move it from the root to your lower spine and into the back part of your backbone, then northward unto the area of your neck, further to your crown and forward across your face, down through your throat and through your heartseal, down through your solar plexus and again through your root. This is the circulation.

During the passion of your sexual exchanges, many of you release your energy and this is a limited form - it is linear. It is alright, but it is linear. It is three dimensional. The understanding of a circle in nature is eternal, allowing the energy to continue moving and never stopping its flow with congestion. In this manner, it will be very, very powerful. It will decongest any of the areas where you now sense congestion. When it is balanced with the maleness and femaleness in harmony, it is very powerful. It is cosmic joy, the ecstasy of God exhibited through creation - the creation of all of life. The circulation of energy allows the course to change. When you find yourself in a passionate embrace, merely contemplate the circular movement of the energy. You may release it. Release it, but also at the same time allow the circulation to be within you, this rebalances your Self.

You know, many of you have a passion for sweets, or for starches or even for your tobacco. Do you know all of this is feminine in nature - this foodstuff? Meat and heavier proteins are your male essence foodstuffs. If you have passion for one or the other, then that is the soul essence rebalancing you through your foodstuffs. When this craving or passion is satisfied, your balance is accomplished. A woman heavy with child having her passions and cravings for certain foods is rebalancing the hormones that are changing within her system. That is why there is a desire for the sour and sweet. The balancing and reharmonizing through unification occurs in all your activities and associations, even foodstuffs. It permeates every facet of your life. Passion for a thing that is outside of you is, in a manner, having a sexual relationship, for you exchange your sexual energies with it and rebalance yourself. This rebalancing may occur at any time.

You may have the union with this universe in ecstasy through passion exhibited by God, without physical sexual exchange, and this will occur when you recourse the energy through you, for what you exchange with is Self with SELF. It is multi-dimensional. It is not only three dimensional in this universe, on this Earth plane. It exchanges and rebalances throughout the time continuum. That is why you have certain of your activities during slumber - you call them dreams. That is why you have erotic dreams. It is sexual energy rebalancing polarities within you at soul essence level through vibrations you can identify.

Passion in any area of your life is merely the fervent desire for the fruition of love, for love expressed. The urge to create. The surge to merge. This creates a focus in the crown seal. That is the channel through to your soul. Through this area your soul is accessible. Shall we call it the soul socket? At any time you may plug into it with your electrical energy known as passion, and access all the power of God unto your unlimited being here on this plane, and you may experience passion in manners which you never knew existed. You may merge with all of creation in the ultimate knowingness of All-That-Is.

When an entity has a passion for creating art, on the canvas or through tones, this exhilarating passion for creating art is divine inspiration accessed in an unlimited manner. It is very possible upon this Earth plane, but you limit yourselves by perceiving that you cannot do this. You think it involves an effort to move into unlimitedness and to circulate the energies. It need not be an effort. It is effortless when allowed, and what is allowance but femininity, the understanding of unconditional love. Allow the feminine aspect of you to come forth and you create passion in a divine manner. The fruit of this is experiencing your God SELF. You say: 'What has passion to do with my becoming aware of the God I Am?' Everything, EVERYTHING! In order to become aware and draw the veil of the God I Am within you, balance is the requirement. The energy exchange of the polarities and the continuity through the completion of the circuit is a requirement. Passion is an energy exchange, is the fervent desire to create life.

Why do you think the male brings forth thrust so instinctively? It is the desire to create life. It is the male aspect in a three dimensional understanding - to be sovereign, to be in control and to create life in an organized fashion. Thrust or surge are the male aspects of sexuality and passion. Femininity is the cooling energy. The absorption of this energy through sexual union is the cooling of the fiery thrust of masculinity. Therefore, the cool assuages the warm, the hot, and they become tepid. They become One through the understanding of God.

The fruit of passion, the olive - both the seed and the pulp create olive oil. What is oil anyway? A lubricant, a balm, a healer. The seed is hard. It creates life through implantation. It is the masculine part of it. The pulp is soft, allowing, digestible, absorbing, beauteous. It is the feminine part, and both create the oil which is the balm unto the soul.

It is by no accident that ninety-nine percent or so of your olive oil in the United States is produced in this area [California] of your country. Why? Because of the emphasis of Christus being brought forward in this area of your country. You are indeed becoming the light unto the world, as you allow your Christus to come forth. And what is Christus? Maleness and femaleness together. Passion exemplified - passion for life, for All That Is.

Questions and answers.

If we look historically at this, we might say that we have had an era of matriarchy, and we have had an era of patriarchy. Would you say that the new age is the age of androgeny?

The age of God, which is neither matriarch, nor patriarch, but both. Androgeny is the culmination of the union indeed.

Within each individual?

Indeed. That is what all archangels are. They are all androgynous, although they may emphasise the masculine or feminine polarity for better identification. They are really androgynous.

So our goal is to become androgynous?

It is not a goal. You already are. You only need to realize it. It is alright if you place emphasis upon maleness or femaleness. There is nothing wrong with this. You only need know that your soul essence is neither. A particular affinity towards maleness or femaleness is divine desire in human free will. There is nothing wrong with it. It allows you to express and experience the polarities with a partner of the opposite gender by merging Self with Self in this manner, for they are merely your mirror. It also enables you to know what masculinity is and femininity is as you embody within that particular focus. *First you experience limited passion through your loins and then you experience unlimited passion through your crown, merged with your heart seal.* It will be a thrust forward from your heart seal, outwardly expanding in all directions from your heart seal, accessing the energy through the channel of your crown rather than the channel of your loins. You will notice, as you come into super-consciousness, that your genitals, the physical apparatus of your sexuality, will become much different in nature. You will still experience sexual merging and you will still have the passion within the loins, but it will be in a different manner, for you will also have the knowingness of passion through your crown. You will not have the emphasis and accrual of desire within the loin area. It will be a balanced desire, a pouring forth in physicality, likened unto the pouring forth in non-physicality.

Birthing also will be in a different manner. It will be without pain. This birthing will be in passion, for it is creating another life force. The fruit of the womb will be your olive, Christ-consciousness - peace, harmony, victory, union. Passion in physical sexuality in super-consciousness will accomplish the merging, but your sexual organs will not appear as they do now. They will not completely atrophy, but they will recede, recede in prominence, in emphasis, in focus. Your embodiments will become more likened unto one another as your essences do, for your embodiment is a result of your essence. You will all feast upon one another in joy and the spirit of communion, in the spirit of reverence of one another and SELF. Is there further query?

St. Germain, could you talk a little bit more about the process of recycling the circular motion of passion?

Would you care to experience it?

Certainly.

Would you all care to experience it?

Indeed.

Place yourself in a comfortable position. Breathe in deeply the air, the life force. Know that you are God, the I Am. Feel deeply into the soul of you, into your loins, feel warmth, heat, passion. Feel it rising. Feel the warmth permeate and circulate in the area of your loins. Feel it vibrating. Feel the vitality of it. Feel the penetrating power of it. Round and round it goes through your loins - hot, hot. Move it up towards your spine. Circulate it around your spine and through your loins, back and forth, warm, loving, warm. Now move it up through your spine, upwards, every vertebrae, hot, heat. Pulsate with the life force within you. Breathe with the pulsation of it, upward, upward, upward to your neck - upward through your crown. Circulate it with emphasis round and round here. Pulsate, vibrate. Now down over your forehead, your third eye, across the top of your face into your throat. Hot. It is like a hot veil being pulled across the top of your face; down into your heart seal. Feel the warmth penetrate your breast, your entire chest cavity. Now down to your solar plexus. Circulate again from your loins [root] up through your spine, through your crown, over your face through your throat, into your heart, down through your solar plexus. Hot, hot. Heat is the answer here. Penetrate with balming, calming warmth. Bring forth calm. Penetrate your loins. Recirculate it all the way around. Continue this circulation. Do not let it stop, for the circulation creates the balance and eternality of your life force. Penetrate your entire embodiment. Let the glow catch fire in this circulation. Fire ignited - burn, burn the entirety of you. Your soul essence is on fire. Expand, expand, become a bonfire. Penetrate, expand, breathe warmth and heat - glow. Become a ball of fire, an eternal, ever-lasting ball of fire. Continue the circulation, expand. You are the Earth. Be in union with the Earth. Pulsate, vibrate, breathe with the Earth. The Earth is fire. You are fire. You are One. You are the cosmos. You are the universe. Be expansive. Continue to be the flame. Continue to be the bonfire. Burn, burn the torch of freedom that you are, the torch of sovereign God. The I Am within you is burning, burn. Come forward in light and love and peace. You are the sparkle of the flame. The flame is within you. You are peace. You are the torch of freedom. Go forward in the light of the universe in your own sovereignty, in your own God I Am.

Now burn quietly, steadily, harmoniously. Breathe heavily. Let the passion recede. Be the everlasting flame, both expansive and focused at once. Refocus this passion again within your breast. You are the God I Am. You are cosmic awareness. You are cosmic joy. You may refocus in this reality as you desire. Breathe deeply.

Now tell me, do any of you feel a subtle difference? There will be more than a subtle difference when you do this during sexual activity. Ask your partner. Your responses will be different. Even your ejaculation will be different. For one thing, the seed will become enlightened. It will have light interspersed within it. It will be less dense.

Did you know that we would have a sexual education class here tonight? You know, when you accomplish passion within you in an unlimited fashion, your embodiment changes. As you focus the energy on your spine, the nerves expand so they may capacitate and handle more energy of a higher charge, more than they do now in third density. The electrums of your nerve endings change. Therefore, they have more capacity to handle your own light as you enlighten yourself. The pituitary gland and the pineal gland are in conjunction and union with your nerve endings and the changes that occur therein.

I focus on sexuality simply because it is the focus of this mass consciousness, but as you experience other manners of passion, you may express it in this way and expand into the passion of the universe in cosmic joy. You will indeed become most inspirational during these times. In your passionate, physical and sexual embrace you will have divine inspiration. It may be frustrating for your mate, but in time they also will have such inspiration as you exchange in this manner. Alright?

You know there is a little tale of the entity that shouted: 'Eureka - I found it.' It is recorded in your history books that this occurred in the tub of the bath. It was not recorded that it was in the tub of the bath in ecstatic union. It would have been quite embarrassing for the entity. Therefore, it was withheld, but this was indeed the case. So, anticipate inspiration. You know what inspiration is? Allowance of your own knowingness, allowance of your divinity. The fruit of passion is merely divinity experienced and known, and you may bite of it and savour it forever. Sink your teeth into it and absorb it with passion.

Go forth now and light the world. Stroke your brushes of passion upon all of creation. The canvas of the universe is yours to paint as you will, to partake of as you will, to ignite as you will. Love the world. Have joy within every expression of creation. Exchange energies with every expression of creation. *Every* expression, the birds' song, the water of your heavens, your lakes, your oceans, your night skies and the twinklings of the stars. Experience it all with an exchange of the energy called passion. *Become* the passion. Once experienced, it is you. So become it. Become the fruit of this passion, aphrodisiac unto yourselves.

I will bid you farewell for now. As I go forth into what you call seventh dimension, seventh plane, I will merge there also with you, for you also are unlimited. There is essence of you that is also seventh dimension, seventh plane, and I will intermingle with your essence and partake of your passion. Explore yourself. Love yourself. Embrace yourself through the mirror of all that is. So be it.

Chapter 6

QUESTIONS & ANSWERS

On soulmates and related topics.

Greetings, my brothers and sisters. Such brilliance - I am honoured to bask within it. How may I help you this day in your time?

Q: St. Germain, a question about soulmates: Are we talking about a constellation of people that form sort of a soul body?

Indeed.

Q: How does that apply to the ascension of an individual?

As you gather more of the soul essence energy unto you, you gather quite naturally more of your Earth plane soulmates unto you. While it may be either male or female in essence and both non-physical and physical in manifestation, it will come unto you as a light energy recognized as of your own essence. When this occurs, it is a natural progression towards enlightenment. It is what you would call maturation in the process of ascension.

Q: Do these souls ascend together?

Indeed. It is not harmonious to do otherwise.

Q: These thirteen masters that you described yourself as part of, are they considered part of that soulmate constellation?

Indeed.

Q: And is that separate from the seven that Mafu and Ramtha talk about?

The seven are part of the thirteen.

Q: Then why is there a distinction?

There need not be. You see, separation assists in the understanding of the mental process. It allows you to gather alignment with what you would term to be technicalities and picking apart of theories, etcetera. It is a progressive understanding - a stepping stone - into unlimitedness where there is no separation, you see?

Q: Is there still a personality essence?

Not once you have come unto the understanding of ascension. For once you are One with the Father/Mother, the Source essence, then there is no such thing as personality, for that is separation in and of itself and limitation. When you are truly unlimited, you are merged and you are one with the void, and you become in knowing of all. In the knowing of All-That-Is, that is you, you know not any separation, for all is reflective of you.

Q: So in essence, we could say that you and Ramtha and Mafu are all the same?

Of course we are. Why consider you that we have such similar phraseology? Being one with the void is a sort of a soul melt. We are all One. When we focus our energy to present ourself in this manner for the gathering of light on this Earth plane, we focus bundles of frequency of energy and those particular frequencies are different in that which you call personality. However, in truth all of us are the same.

Q: So is there a thirteen of each one of us too?

The thirteen is becoming quite a popular subject. You see, as this divine Source, or the Father, issued forth contemplation of itself, it decided and desired more experience and expansion in an area that was physical in nature and denser, more focused. In order to do this, it created thirteen bodies of soul essence. As it did this, there was no differentiation in gender. There was no male or female. There was no personality either. It was simply an amorphous body of energy. As this fragmented in order to experience in physicality and gather that knowingness and garnish the wisdom within it, it came unto the knowingness of male/female, personality, physical, non-physical, etcetera. So, there are many fragmentary understandings, and there are thirteen of these. They are all identical, however, each has one particular frequency that emphasizes a specific resonance for the purpose of synchronization of All-That-Is, in the symphonic understanding of an orchestra. So in order to understand the thirteen, you must know that they are all identical in nature, and each one of you belongs to one of the thirteen, however, all of the thirteen also belong to the Source, or the Father, and the merging with that is called ascension. In ascending, you become one with All-That-Is, and one with these thirteen that you are so curious about, and one with all that is your soulmate essence and your singular body of energy of the thirteen.

Q: Could we be fragmented into more than thirteen, or more than twenty, or..?

Within each one of the thirteen, there are thousands. As you gather your energy unto you, you will all merge together back into the One and then this One will merge with all the other thirteen. Then you will go unto the void. It is part of the fifth and sixth density progression. You may do this in a moment - in the twinkling of an eye. It takes no time at all, for there is no time in that dimension, as time is a limitation.

Q: What is the grand thought that you think of merging into?

Love.

Q: And where did the seven come from? And who are the other six?

The other six - they have no personality, my brother. It is not a who, it is a what, and that is God.

Q: How about the seven, how did that start?

The seven in your understanding are merely the essences of this body of energy who desire to come forward in this manner in what you would call a package deal, hm? You see, there is nothing special about these particular seven. It was merely a particular desire of theirs to come forward in this manner. The other six are not left behind. They merely have other desires. It is all divine. In the eternal unfoldment, you are in the embryonic stage, and that which you consider to be I would be in grammar school. So you see, we are all mirrors to each other. We are all unfolding in our own knowingness.

Q: St. Germain, does each of the thirteen oversouls resonate to a particular colour?

Indeed, for colour is merely frequency.

Q: What frequency are you in colour?

Violet. Do you understand what violet represents?

Q: Christ-consciousness?

Indeed. The balance - divine balance of unconditional love and sovereignty, unconditional love represented on your planet by that colour known as pink. Sovereignty is the colour of blue. The merging of the two is violet.

Q: St. Germain, would you comment on the importance of that other part of the soul, the soulmate, also demonstrating on this plane - the coming together of the two?

You see, that which is soulmate in essence is not necessarily upon this plane, although it very well may be. It is not necessary to merge with it physically. The merging will occur automatically anyway, and when the physical merging occurs, if it so should, then it will be unlike anything you have experienced thus far. It will be experienced in fourth density and I will tell you this: The physical merging in super-consciousness will only be with a soulmate, and it will be celebration at all times. Indeed. It will be the igniting and sparking of soul essence in communion and in love expressed to one another.

Q: Is that why so many soulmate couples are having problems now, because they are not in fourth density?

That is part of it. They are affected by third density interruption, as you would call it.

Q: If they were more in fourth density, then they would experience more harmony?

Indeed. They are also unfolding into complete fourth density themselves. They are in transition. At times they are fourth. At times they are third. At times they are a bit of both. When super-consciousness prevails, there will be peace and harmony and joy. It will indeed be a sparking place.

Q: Members of that soulmate constellation who may be lagging behind - are they automatically brought up by the efforts of the rest of the group?

If they so desire, which generally speaking they do. There is an occasional occurrence of an inward collapse with certain entities who are not desirous of going forward into the alignment of the rest of the soul essence. When this occurs, it is like being without a limb. However, it is quite possible - there is nothing that is not possible - to go forward into the All-That-Is without this particular electrum that was involved in an inward collapse. That is merely the black hole of a soul essence. This occurred with the grand entity Ramtha.

Q: And is that eventually reparable?

This is of which I speak. It is very probable that this soul can come forward out of the black hole, the inward collapse, and come into the Source. However, in the case of Ramtha it has not been done, but it is possible. Ramtha came forward in the knowingness of All-That-Is in the contemplation of nature, in the contemplation of pain, in the contemplation of warrior and victim. In all of this he came into the knowing of freedom and love. There was part of this essence that was his female soulmate and desired to experience inward collapse. This grand entity Ramtha went forward anyway and came into the understanding of All-That-Is. This particular part of the electrum that was remaining still remains. It is not impossible, however, for it to come forward and merge.

Q: That is true of Mafu too?

Indeed.

Q: So is the woman who channels Ramtha the part that remains?

No. This entity that is the instrument is not the soul essence of the grand entity Ramtha. It was merely very dear and adored and beloved of the essence called Ramtha.

Q: St. Germain, does the black hole have to do with Jehovah?

Indeed. It has much to do with Jehovah, it has also much to do with the grand diseasement called AIDS. That diseasement is the understanding of physical man, the denseness of man much likened unto Sodom and Gomora. It is for the realization of superficiality, of that which is not of the heart seal, but of the root seal; and brings forward that which is not of Christ-consciousness, but of Alter Ego in nature. As the two confront, one either resolves this and comes into the knowingness of All-That-Is within oneself and allows that light to heal, or one allows the Alter Ego to express as this diseasement, which is an attraction to clinging to third density. This is the experience of misalignment, pain, disharmony, remorse, regret, and sorrow. As this is experienced, one is in desolation and joy ceases from one's being. This is what is desired by the Alter Ego - to cling to third density.

Alter Ego does not exist in non-physical realms. Only in the physical does it exist, for only in the physical is it separate from the Divine Ego of SELF, and it fears everything for it knows it not. It fears to go unto the light, to merge with the light of you, to allow the light to seep into you. As it does, it becomes threatened, because it does not know what will occur. It is like a child. This also applies to Jehovah. Feeling unconditional love for the Alter Ego and Jehovah, the Alter Ego will recede in aggressiveness. It will succumb to love. It will tame itself. It will be solaced, assuaged and loved, for as you speak unto it and allow it to know that it truly is loved, it is part of you, then it will know that it will be loved even when it is within the light, for the light will love it even more so. Talk to it as you talk to a child, for it truly behaves and responds like a child of you that is not knowing and afraid and does not understand. This is alright, for when the merging occurs, you are truly aligned and balanced, the Alter Ego becomes sovereign and the unconditional love that assuaged it becomes the unconditional love of all of life, the whole of life; and as you merge the two, you become God.

Q: Often there is a conflict about responsibility to family members, because it is not their truth that one should walk away from responsibility.

What is responsibility but slavery unto another? You see, each entity is sovereign unto itself. Each divine essence is responsible only for itself and this is all. You may indeed be in harmony with your family without being in agreement. You see, this is allowance in true form - to allow what you disagree with to be in its own divinity. You may love them and love them heartily, unconditionally, but do not be in slavery unto them because of responsibility. Obligation or the burden of responsibility is submission unto another's sovereignty and this is not harmonious with the unfoldment into light.

Q: Well, my child is a mother with two young children and how would a mother be sovereign with two children? She has chosen to help them in their growth until they can maintain themselves.

How is it you consider the entity Mary was sovereign with Jesus? In your understanding of limitation called third density, you will allow them what is called passageway and corridor rather than a box. In the allowance of their sovereignty, you also issue forth your own and when you do this, there is the desire for mutual respect and mutual love. This is how all essences will respond to one another in super-consciousness.

This is how children of your plane in the transition of third to fourth density - or limited into unlimited understanding - are being assisted in their understanding: The allowance of the sovereignty of their parents, and their parents in allowance of their sovereignty. Mutual mirrors, mutual respect and love. You may all be grand examples to one another in this manner. As you do so, you light your own flame.

Q: I have had many different relationships - some very intense where I thought I was in love. How can I come to terms with my life?

First of all, my dear, the many entities you encounter in this life experience are your mirror, so that you may know this is not where your happiness lies. *It is you.* Be not in sorrow of the ending of relationships. It is to be in joy of, for in this joy you are realizing every moment that what is taken away from you and what you would desire to have, is not outward of you. It is inward of you. They are merely the reflectors and as they pass away, you do not see yourself, and you feel at a loss. As they go into other experiences, you feel then that part of you has been dissolved, and it truly has not, for you are All-That-Is, you are infinite. It is never-ending. It is expressed in all manner and form. Indeed, these entities have come unto you in your past for you have desired to learn this before. You have become hard-headed as it were, and did not get it and you are desirous of doing so this time, most especially since you are coming more into the light of other dimensional parts of you. The entities that are mirroring you are not the only relationships. Consider it, my dear. It is all about you in your close intimate contact.

You create all of your circumstances, but in this particular disharmonious relationship, the intense nature of it is the reverberation and vibration of your soul's desire to know that your joy is your own soul essence in harmony and alignment with All-That-Is. Your joy truly does not lie outward in whatever experience, success, or in a relationship with an entity, or with children, for that is giving your sovereignty away. Your joy and happiness is your sovereignty. Give it not to another entity to have sovereignty over you. To have the direction of whither you go and how you perceive yourself emanates from within, from the knowingness here in your soul, within your breast. It pulsates here. That is why you feel heartbroken. You do not know that yet.

Q: St. Germain, it seems that the times when I have a skin rash is when I am in a relationship. Is this an indication of something that is being cleared out or..?

The rash upon your skin is simply because of the fear you have of the relationship. It is not the relationship itself that you fear, but the other entity - the other gender of SELF. It is fear of your Alter Ego, clinging to this Earth plane. It desires to cling, for it sees that there is much light within you, and therefore it presents itself more and more fearful. This Earth plane, this physicality, is the only place that the Alter Ego is demonstrated. There is no other place where separation is known. It is merged and unified in harmony elsewhere in the non-physical. So as your essence is more and more illuminated it harbours within itself the fervent desire to cling and in doing so it presents more and more disruption of SELF in order to misalign so that there will be less light. It feels uncomfortable within light. In order to align it, all you need do is allow it to know that it is loved of the light. The Alter Ego is indeed very childlike, very much like an infant that does not understand, that is fearful.

The response required to align it is very similar to how you would respond to a child that has fear of the unknown. The unknown can be very terrorizing for a child, can be very much of a nightmare and so it is for the Alter Ego. This outbreak of a rash upon the skin is merely one form in which it presents itself. It is the misalignment of the light within your being exhibited through your skin. Your skin is becoming immersed and interspersed with light - it itself is becoming lighter. You will notice this among many entities upon your plane - the skin will become lighter and lighter. Third density infiltrates the light of your skin and presents what you call rash. All that you may do is come into the harmonious understanding of the causation of it. Then you may draw unto you the mate of your being, and in this exchange of life force, that relationship, there will be no rash.

On bodily changes.

Q: St. Germain, lately I have a lot of occurrences in my body - like my heart speeds up, my body becomes very hot, my ears plug up and there is an extreme pressure in my head. I also experience remembrances, like suddenly remembering something - similar to waking up from a dream.

What you are experiencing is the alteration of the embodiment. The plugging up of the ears is merely your consciousness not allowing you to respond to third density in your auditory and oral capacity. Your senses do not desire to partake of third density, for the knowingness of the senses beyond the physical will allow you to come into the light of the knowingness of what you are. That which is the aching of the head and the congestion and all of this - I have explained that unto you as applicable to unfoldment. However, this which is experienced like a dream - it is not dream. It appears as fantasy within your slumber, but it is an experience of the fifth density other you of which you are becoming aware. That is why you have physical manifestations of discomfort. Your embodiment is readjusting to the re-entry into fifth density consciousness by realigning third to fourth.

Q: Sometimes it is such an overwhelming energy it feels as though I have to pass out. What do I do when this occurs?

The speeding up of your embodiment, of your systems, is your metabolism increasing in frequency. It is quite natural. What you may do to align it is breathe heartily. Allow the electrums of the atmosphere to enter your lungs and filtrate it within your heart, within your heart seal - that which is love. That will enable the circulatory system of you to dispense a calming, that which is loving. It will slow down your metabolism to the point where it is harmonious with your embodiment at this point in your time. So breathe it in, allow the light to enter it and then pulsate it throughout your embodiment. As it carries oxygen to the cells of your embodiment, it will also carry light. So the light will remain, but it will remain in harmony and not disharmony.

Q: St. Germain, I recall having had an experience during which the body felt as if the energy was racing through it at such a high speed that it seemed to dissolve, yet I was still aware that it was there, but my awareness seemed to expand into a realm that was totally allowing for the knowledge of who I was. What had occurred?

All things occur because you desire them to occur. It was an allowance in the moment of unfolding into the Source. That was perceived physically as a current, electromagnetic energy magnified. It was the flowing forward of the All-That-Is. As you expand unto the All-That-Is, and allow your soul essence and the light body to come unto you, you will experience this more and more and it will envelop your entire auric field. You will feel aglow. You will feel electrified. As you do this, you may touch an item and you will sear it. You will char it. Touching people, you will leave an imprint upon them.

Consider the shroud of Turin of the man Jesus in this context. It will occur also with you and this was an enlightening taste of what will occur.

On colours.

Q: Could you expand on healing colours?

Colour in essence does not heal. The heart and the love energy coming from that heart do the healing. Colour is really extraneous. It really matters not. Indeed, the true source of all healing, whether it be physical in nature or of soul essence or planetary in nature, is the essence that issues forth from your heart seal, the divine Source. When colour is used in healing, it merely emphasizes one or another particular manner of healing, but if you would send forth what is golden in essence, it will be all-encompassing. It is unlimited in the healing, regardless of the focal point. It will heal multi-dimensionally.

Q: Will white not do the same thing?

White is golden without the glow. Indeed, white is the combination of all colours. You see, when you look at an ancient portrait, there is a golden aura above those that are understood as saintly. That is because the essence of their etheric being, of their light body, is golden in nature. That is how it is perceived, and many essences and entities in that time in your history perceived auric fields. Many of your painters were very inspirational. They were very much channels, as you term them to be now in your time, and they painted what they saw. That is why your metal called gold is so precious in your day and time. It is very likened unto Christ-consciousness in and of itself. It is soft, gentle, glowing, warm and healing. Quite naturally it would be valued in your society or any society for that matter; and it will continue to be valued in super-consciousness when it prevails upon this plane.

On name changes.

Q: I have heard that people get the name of their soul. Is that the name of their oversoul?

Here we go with names! Your soul essence as it is merged with the Source has no name, for it has no personality. It is One with the Source, you see. So your spiritual name or whatever, is for the amusement of you at this particular time.

Q: So you can choose any one you want?

One that vibrates unto your essence as you are at this point in your time. You have had many third density names in your different life experiences upon this plane. You also have many fourth density names, for in your simultaneous experience on other dimensions of expression, you are fourth density multitudinous times. If you desire a title or a name, choose one with which you resonate at this point in your unfoldment. As you progress further, that will change over and over again, until it dissipates into no name, into that which is One with all. There are myriads of light reflections upon this plane coming forth in this manner to appease you. Reflecting on past lives is also an appeasement. It is alright. There is nothing wrong with this. This appeasement is quite third density in nature. That is alright. However, a soul name is not truly a soul name - it is a misnomer.

On St. Germain.

Q: St. Germain, in your last time on this Earth plane here, what were you doing right before the big..

Jackpot, hm? At the time I was gazing at the sun and I was contemplating the gloriousness of it. I became one with the stardust, the crystalline water and the mountains which were draping the sun. I was in love with it all. I was so in awe and so amazed by the beauty before my eyes that my tears fell unto the cheeks - I became the water, I became the sun, I became the stardust within the sky and I also became the wind and all of life, the trees, the birdsong, the cricket cry. I became it all and I merged and contemplated the All-That-Is, the Oneness. I desired to return hence unto this plane to bring more knowingness to the entities abiding on this plane, those who did not understand the light, who were not aware. I desired to draw the veil a little to allow light to filter in. I came as Le Comde St. Germain to bring this understanding to the governments of Europe, to the inner Earth plane and to the brothers of beyond. You call them your space brothers. They call you their space brothers. Indeed, I was in communion with all of them.

As I brought forth some of the light, they exemplified their human free will and many of them gave me what you call a 'deaf ear'. This is alright. It is all divine. There is nothing wrong with this at all, but it altered the plan a bit. As we came forward, and I say 'we' because there were more at this point - not only I - as we came forward with more desire to enlighten your Earth plane, we hearkened upon the understanding of your grand nation [U.S.A.], your new Jerusalem - the birthplace of Christ-consciousness. This continent, it was truly birthed in freedom and equality and the founding fathers are now known as the Brotherhood; and the thirteen original colonies, guess what: Each one of the thirteen soul essences was represented. Jesus and the twelve disciples were also thirteen. Each one has resonance to a particular frequency and so also has each one of the colonies resonance to its identical frequency.

Q: St. Germain, when you are asked a question that is not directly part of your experience, how is it that you can respond?

The merging of the heart seals allows that knowingness to be one with that which is I.

Q: So in a sense, basically you are reading cellular memory?

I am not reading it. I know it.

Q: Knowing the cellular memory and acting as the mirror of it.

Indeed. This is exactly how it is. You call it a reading. We do not resemble a book at all. I reflect that knowingness back unto you.

Q: St. Germain, do you see through those eyes?

I have vision of the third eye as I gaze upon all of you - I see your light. As I focus with these eyes, I see your embodiment, but I see mostly your light. I focus merely so that you will gain recognition that I am responding unto you.

Q: St. Germain, do you see our light as different hues, brighter or dimmer or in different colours?

Of course. Brilliance would issue forth as a combination of white and golden. The auric field of your etheric body is acknowledged from time to time. However, it changes. According to the subject matter, the topic of discussion, your auric fields are constantly in flux. As certain entities become excited about a particular question and their ears perk, their auric field charges and changes. If an entity dozes, as their conscious awareness dissipates, their auric field changes also. Their etheric light will bring forth green and emerald in hue, and blue, likened unto the sky. The entities who become excited have a tinge of red about them and orange, indeed.

Entities who are harmonic - floating as it were, as upon a cloud - they have much of a purple hue about them. The entities who are totally in love with the reflection that I am presenting of themselves, they have much pink about them. You see, what they love is not I - it is they. Indeed, I perceive that as a secondary impression to the white and golden and as I focus even more, I would perceive your physical presentation. I express much warmth and much hearty appreciation for this experience.

Q: St. Germain, how far does our auric field extend past our body?

All are different. As you compare one unto another, you are separating yourselves. Generally speaking, with third density awareness about you - the to and fro of third and fourth density knowingness within you and the battle of Armageddon occurring within you - in this state the auric field generally extends about five or six of your feet past your embodiment. But this is it in totality - in all its levels of understanding, all its frequencies. There are times in your state of meditation or contemplation that it is truly extended ad infinitum. There are times when during heat and anger and your fits of frustration it becomes a bit narrower than this, for it is concentrated on third density - it is grosser, denser, but these limits will soon dissipate from your contemplation, as you progress into an understanding of unlimitedness.

On dolphins and whales.

Q: St. Germain, dolphins are with soul. Are they without Alter Ego?

No, but they are in alignment with it. They were upon your plane in the time of Atlantis, but they were not Atlanteans, they were Lemurians in nature. They were very close to the spiritual essence. Their nature is the love of life, joy and laughter, and the civilization of Atlantis was not harmonious to them. Atlantis was very technological, very war-like, very much in desire of ruling and having dominion over all the rest of the Earth and her peoples. The Lemurians were conquered by the Atlanteans and brought into submission. They gave love unto the Atlanteans and insight into the divinity of All-That-Is, of all the entities that abided within your plane at that point in your time. However, after the fall of Atlantis they came forward again, in a different embodiment, and they chose water as their abode. The dolphin is truly of another planetary understanding.

Q: I have heard Mafu say the dolphins will be leaving this density and most of them would be returning to the Pleiades. Are there other beings who will choose not to be there but somewhere else, when the Earth makes her transition to fourth density? And who might they be?

Your whales. Why do you think there was so much commotion about saving the whales? They truly are your brothers. Their beachings and their moaning is merely the crying out to their brothers [humans] to allow them to know the communion between the two of them. They know this. The peoples upon the land do not know this. The whales suicided in masses merely to reach out to their brethren, and yet they understood not - the peoples upon the land. They truly understood not. They will.

Q: Thank you. One other thing, when you mention the dolphins, tremendous emotion wells up in me. (Agreement from others).

Many of you have been present in Lemuria and Atlantis and you are not only in communion with them, many of you have part of your soul essence in that understanding. That is why there is such affinity to the dolphin now in your time, when super-consciousness is appearing on the horizon. The dolphins have been rather submissive in nature. They will become more aligned with the balance of sovereignty and unconditional love, and will become the mirror for humanity.

On meditation.

Q: St. Germain, do you have a meditation for raising the kundalini to the crown chakra?

Meditation can become ritualistic. It is grand indeed to go forth into this contemplation of quietude and the solitude within SELF. It is indeed helpful and assisting third density transition to fourth. However, we would desire for it not to become a dogma, for that is limitation. However, as you progress into the unfoldment of fourth density or super-consciousness, or ascension, then you will know that your life is a meditation. You will walk in a constant meditation. In your beingness, you will be God. Therefore, meditation is unnecessary. However, we do allow you the amusement of it.

Miscellaneous.

Q: St. Germain, You said there is some female energy of the Council of Thirteen, that may come - is Matea one of those?

I understand of which you speak. However, I wish you to know that a personality or gender in this manner is really for your purposes.

Q: I understand.

Not all entities do. That which you consider to be I is both male and female in total alignment. In truth I am neither, for I am both. The purpose of the entity of which you speak, coming forward in a female presentation, is for the understanding of equality upon your plane. As she comes, mankind, not womankind, will understand that womankind is also sovereign and will be very much surprised, truly surprised. Matea is very much a part of the essence that will issue forward, however, there is also the female part of the entity which has been known as Jeshua.

Q: Is that Reena?

That is part of the fragmentary understanding that it has been known as. The fragmentary understanding of what you know of as I has been known as Merlin, also as Christopher Columbus and many other entities. Reena is also a life experience that is known as part of this energy. However, it will take many by surprise. You see, there are many things of which your plane is not aware at this point in time, and those are the things your Book of Revelation refers to as 'bewares'.

Q: We are supposed to beware?

No, for there is nothing to fear. However, those essences that do fear, will create much trepidation about the birthing of a particular male essence that is to come, because they do not contemplate a female essence. Yet female essence is unconditional love, demonstrating Christ-consciousness through the unconditional love of the nature of woman. This, combined with sovereignty, will truly personify Christ-consciousness. They did not contemplate this.

Q: This entity will be born?

It appears that this will occur at this point in your time [1987]. All is subject to change. There have been many radical changes in the consciousness of this plane. Therefore, there are alterations in the design and desires of the ones who are here to assist those upon this plane.

Q: Should we look for a star in the heavens?

Gaze at all of them, for the star [[of Bethlehem] was not a star. It was a craft.

Q: Is the entity that we know of as Mary, of the group of oversouls?

That indeed was one of the thirteen who had presentation on this Earth. It is a bit different than Jeshua - or Sananda, or any of the other names this entity is known as. You see, the energy known as Sananda, or Jesus, is known heartily upon other planes as well, not only on this Earth. You know the entity Jesus also by the terminology you call Krishna. It was another essence or fragment, but it really matters not, for you are all as divine as these entities. We are all Krishna. We are all Jesus. We are all quite capable of exemplifying Christ-consciousness in personification as an example in physicality - mirror to all the rest of life. Indeed.

Q: St. Germain, so then Jesus is part of the Great White Council as well - am I understanding that correctly?

Indeed.

Q: Alright, now, the scriptures talk about his return in the sky. How is that - is that Christ-consciousness or is that to be a physical thing?

First of all, there are multi-dimensional meanings here. There is the physical embodiment of a particular essence that represents Christ-consciousness, as many will upon this plane - not only one entity, but many, but it will be in the form of an embodiment. It will not be coming out of nothingness, for there is a craft above that which you perceive to be a cloud. Christ-consciousness will be descending and it will be assisted from above, from the unseen. What do you think the Brotherhood is, hm? They are also your brothers from space. They are at present of the unseen, and they are issuing forth Christ-consciousness on your plane, for they understand the adventures of humankind and the stumbling blocks they create for themselves. You see, the Brotherhood and the brothers of the unseen from space, watch you and what they see can be likened unto gazing on mice in a maze. They watch them come to barriers, sniff around a bit, turn around and fall into another barrier; and sniff around a bit and go in circles and become puzzled; and eventually they find their way out if they trouble themselves enough. At times they end up from where they started. However, this is the journey humanity has chosen for itself and there is no judgment at all. Your brothers from above and the Grand White Brotherhood are very allowing of this and very loving.

Q: St. Germain, I do not have a sense of home - home seems to be wherever I am. So I sit here, I look around, and I know that if I want to work I can just manifest it. Then when I get beyond that thought it feels like it is just another distraction, and I am so caught up in the distractions that it keeps me from just doing anything..

It is only conflict because you let third density get in your way. The desire to make progress or understand it all is merely the finite of you desiring to have a look at it under a microscope. Your feeling that home is wherever you are is the experience of unlimitedness in the moment. Truly desire the joy of the moment and do not contemplate what will come beyond - indeed, this is *being*.

Experience being *you* in the joy of the moment of God, of the God that is *you*, experience all of life in the moment as it appears. Doing this, you will unfold even more and more. Consternation about your progress, your desire to know and understand how it all works, is limitation. It is providing you with frustration. This is all well and wondrous indeed. However, if you would desire the harmonious trip, as it were, simply be in beingness and when this presents itself as a frustration, merely let it be and tell the Alter Ego, it is alright to be frustrated. Acknowledge that this frustration is part of you and let it abide. As it abides, assure it that it is loved for it is part of you and that it also may be in the joy of the moment. The separate parts of you are all one. They will come into the awareness of this unity as you consciously acknowledge that they are one and not separate, not to be fought, confronted, released, forgotten or pushed away. Regarding your home - it is not a place. It is a knowingness. That is why you feel so comforted wherever you are.

Q: But I feel like I am just marching in time - going somewhere but not going anywhere in a sense.

But you still unfold. These frustrations within your being in your desire to be unlimited is further unfoldment, for you are coming into the knowing of it, allowing the light to seep into the third density of you that remains. You are as the mole coming from darkness into the light - the eyes are adjusting and the soul essence is adjusting as well. This soul essence that is adjusting consists not only of the other parts of you that are upon this plane, but also of those parts of you that are of other dimensions. It is all part of the process of coming into the knowing of the divine essence within you. In your dream state during slumber you also assimilate and unfold.

Q: Well, how does destiny then fit in? Did I come here with a specific plan? Is there a specific place in which I am supposed to be?

Destiny is non-existent in an unlimited understanding. Desires are of your soul essence in the moment, and they change moment by moment. Destiny is never cast in stone and can be changed at any time. Desire is merely contemplation of access to third density involvement in order to experience and, therefore, to garner the wisdom contained within the heart and core of that experience. Each moment is wondrous. Each moment is equally valid to every other moment. It is filled with the joy, if you will only partake of it.

Q: St. Germain, whose outrageous fantasy is this separation?

The God who created all of you, which is *you* in your grander essence. The creative energy of All-That-Is will allow any expression with any circumstance to experience outward awareness of consciousness in third density. It is the desire for what is physical in nature and to understand what it is to be the slayer and the slayee, to be victim and persecutor. You see, life is balanced in that you experience it all, the discord and disharmony. However, when you realign this with the light, knowing that there is a divine message contained within, then you are garnering it, then you have known what it is to experience this. You become the knowingness and you relinquish the experience - you give it up into All-That-Is. You bring it forward into other than third density limitation. You allow it to become unlimited, for in doing this you have owned it. That is the grand design for that which is called the madness.

Sometimes it appears in such a way that you ask yourself how could we ever have chosen this? Many of the choices occur at soul essence level, and not at conscious awareness level. The birthing process, the choice of your parents and circumstances surrounding it, that is also the choice of your soul essence. Outward awareness does not permit the knowing of the soul essence to come forward, for that would mean being in unlimitedness. If this were to occur, you would have much confusion upon your plane - that is if you would consciously know of all your other dimensional experiences in the simultaneity of all time. You would not be clear about which experience was within this dimension. Some have called it being insane, schizophrenic in some terminology. Some would call it multiple personality. Some of this is awareness of other expressions of existence. They are not mad. They are unlimited.

You know, Einstein was perceived as mad. Many of your visionaries have been perceived as insane at times. However, the knowingness of your other dimensions in misalignment, in confusion, will manifest disharmonious circumstances which will cause those essences around you to judge you in this manner. It is for the purpose of one's Self to align again. It is also for purposeful good. All is for purposeful good within your experience, within all essences' experience - even though we may not perceive the good outwardly and consciously.

Q: St. Germain, When you speak of living in those different planes simultaneously - for instance, a middle Earth and say on another planetary system - in how many planes can one be living while being embodied on the physical Earth?

If you would desire to count it, you would desire to limit it, for it is constantly in fluctuation and it is infinite.

Q: And as we live in these other dimensions, we evolve and learn on those dimensions also?

Of course.

Q: I also wanted to know about the predictions in regard to earthquakes. Is this something we will need to experience, or..

That is for you as a totality of consciousness to decide and that is constantly in a state of ebb and flow. You see, prediction or projection of what will occur is based upon the now moment if all remains the same - if no one changes their mind at all, which is highly unlikely to say the least. The grand quakers and tremors, the spewing mountains and the grand waves - indeed, at times it appears that this is very likely to occur very soon. However, there are times when that has dissipated in the flow of love of humankind in harmony. These are the moments when many of you are in meditation. During this period of time, there is healing and solacing of the desire for dire circumstance. The only one who truly knows how it will occur is each entity in and of itself, for it is in knowing of its own desires. If you truly do not desire dire circumstance to occur, simply be in the constant knowingness that it will not, that it is nothing to fear; and if there is nothing to fear then truly there will be nothing to fear as result of the divine thought bringing it into manifestation. If you know that humankind are brothers aligned hand-in-hand and heart-in-heart, then this is how it will be in your days to come. That knowing will bring it into manifestation. If you know there is a great tremor or quake coming, then it will.

I will bid you farewell for now, and as I do so, I would desire for each of you to come into knowingness that you are stars in your own right - glowing, heartily glistening, becoming the enigma that others gaze upon; for in that, they are seeing themselves. Blessed be all of you stars. Blessed be the heaven that you call this plane. Blessed be the life that abides within.

Farewell.

Chapter 7

I AM FREE.

Greetings my beloved brothers and sisters, and how are you this day in your time?

Audience: Splendid, brilliant.

Brilliant. You are learning. Indeed, you are all brilliant in your essences. Yet you do not perceive your brilliance, your illumination within the heavens that you call your Earth plane. So you come hence unto this mirror that you may understand what it is to be freedom exemplified, personified, to be God unfettered. What is freedom? Tell me.

Not having limitations?

That is the limited perception of freedom. I will tell you this. There is a grand bird that soars with magnificent beauty and splendour, the eagle, indeed a symbol of freedom. Now, this bird, it knows the limitations, the boundaries, the barriers of Earth, the water and the mountain. Indeed, it perceives these barriers to experience them and to love them. Therefore, it has the freedom to soar with joy and exhilaration. It is indeed the captain of the skies. Why? Because it understands, it loves and it allows the barriers, so it is not lack of limitation. *It is knowing and understanding and embracing limitation.* You see? That is the unlimited understanding of freedom.

Now, on this Earth plane, you have many of your spiritual endeavours and exercises in the fervent attempt to gain access to the knowingness of freedom; but they all call you away from your physicality. You desire to be etheric, but the understanding of physicality gains invalidity in this manner. It is no longer valid to be human. To be earthly, to be physical, is no longer understood as

123

divine, so you walk with your heads in the clouds, literally, and search for freedom there - in the air.

Do you know, every atom within your physicality is pulsing and rushing to the freedom of God essence within it? It is *within* you. It is not without you! This out here is always the mirror for what is in here - always! If you experience and perceive limitation and barriers, it is because you know it in here. It is because you have not embraced the barriers within you.

I will tell you a story. There is a grand mountain. Its peak is covered in snow. It is beauteous and splendid and all who gaze upon it are in awe of it. So you come upon this mountain and you perceive: 'Aha, there is a trail unto the summit. I will climb this mountain and upon the top of it, there is freedom with a capital 'F'. I will know no boundaries. I will be limitless. I can fly and soar into the air. I will owe it to myself to know freedom and I will have earned it so it will be mine.' You enter this pathway and you travail and labour fervently over the rocks and barriers in your path, but this is alright. You know that you have found the pathway to freedom. It is yours. There is no other way, indeed. You call it a thing - probably after yourself. Then you hear an entity somewhere in the distance and they say to you: 'I have found the path to freedom. It is here.' And you reply: 'No, it is here. You are wrong.' You say none other than your own path is right. You do not understand the exuberance that they have upon their travel of their own pathway. Then you encounter a grand boulder within your pathway and you do not understand it. It is an obstacle to you and you become frustrated and flounder for a while of your time. Then you perceive another path. You say: 'Aha, perhaps I was wrong. Perhaps this is the pathway. I shall travel on this one for a while.'

You do thus, and many of you become fatigued from your labour and you opt out by leaving your embodiment. Then you return unto parents who have a pathway of their own on the other side of the mountain. It is indeed disorienting for you. Your parents' pathway is so unfamiliar to you at times, that you become very frustrated with life in its entirety. It is a very common occurrence on your plane for parents and siblings to have unfamiliarity with each others' pathways. Many times it is so disorienting to you that you travel around the mountain, round and round over and over again, viewing all the different pathways at the same level, wondering indeed if there is even a mountain and if there is, if you would desire a pathway at all. You see?

You know, the closer you get to the top of it, the closer all the pathways come together. They converge at one apex, at the summit. Then you may perceive thousands of pathways and understand the validity of each in its own Isness. Each one is the path to freedom. Each one is understood in the joy and magnificence of its own Isness. Some are grassy; some are sandy; some are smooth; some are craggy - but they are all beauteous. As you reach the top of the mountain, you understand what it is to be free. You understand sovereignty and support. Mountain - its symbol is support - solidity, stability. It exists in its own quiet divine knowingness. It does not desire to be elsewhere. It does not desire to be something else. It understands and embraces all its boundaries called pathways. It does not desire to be without them. It does not run and flee hence from it, but rejoices in it, for it is comprised of separate components called boundaries. It supports life grandly. It has life scurrying all about it - the birds, the deer, children, humanity. It permits the experience called life in whatever form it takes to experience freedom. Become the mountain. Become sovereign. Become support. Become allowance. Then you become freedom.

Now, freedom is not fleeing or running from responsibility or hiding your head in the sand as it were, or discounting your experience here. That is not freedom. Freedom is experienced only in the union of the aspects of the wholeness. When you are free, you know it all. You experienced it all, you embrace it all! There are no separations that are invalid. They are all wondrous.

The God I Am essence comes forth on this plane to understand itself through separation of itself.

In doing this, it experiences focus of emotion and then fading out of the focus into the wholeness again. How can you be free if you do not even know from what it is you would desire to be free? Escape induces fear - fear of an aspect that you would consider would limit you, fetter you, bind you; but *it* does not do it, *you* do it. Lie upon the freshly-cut sod of your Earth and gaze up into the heavens and see God. It reflects itself back unto you constantly, but you do not see it. *You are God.* When everything is understood as part of the whole - the physical atoms of your embodiment, your daily activity, your life, your family, your relationships, even your business houses, your busiment of the embodiment - all that - then it gives you the freedom to operate within it. For you understand the aspects so that you may merge them. You cannot merge them if you do not allow them, if you do not affirm their beingness, if you do not understand them and appreciate them. How can you merge them into the whole if you deny them?

Denial is fear. Denial is separation. Denial is further focus into the physicality and less unto the freedom of which I speak. You desire to be free of responsibility - many of you. 'Oh, but if I did not have thus, then I could be free'. Does this sound familiar? You know, if you did not have 'thus', you would not understand what it is to love unconditionally and to allow others to experience as they so choose. Allow them their sovereignty and then you free them. They are no more dependent on you than you on them. Giving them this freedom to be responsible as it were, unto themselves, is the gift of God. As you give them this gift of God, multiplied, it is likened unto the stars within the firmament of being and it becomes illumination and light unto the world. I speak not only of entities, I speak of situations, circumstances, encounters, relationships, everything! Free it. Give it its sovereignty to be confused if it so desires, to be indeed rampant with limitation. It is alright. This is of which I speak.

Limitation is an aspect of God with as much validity as unlimitedness. For without the two, you do not have the whole. The colour of violet is representative of the freedom of the new age, the era of God. You know, violet would not be violet without all its elements - red, white and blue. Red and blue would create a deep purple. White and red creates pink. White and blue creates azure, pastel, none of which is violet. *All* the aspects - limited as they are in their vibration - create the wholeness. Without its composites wholeness would not be and there would not be any freedom. You are the mountain. You exist within the separations and boundaries within you. Your plane is manifested and is created upon the premise of separation. You do not live within one another's skin, do you? You have separate embodiments from one another and separate consciousnesses from one another. Recognizing this allows you to perceive the divinity within this separation, for you are multi-faceted aspects of the prismatic understanding of God I Am. Without the prism of it, it would not be complete.

You all come here to gaze into one another's soul essence, to perceive God, to respect and admire this limited perception of you in physicality. Then release it, do not sever it, do not separate it, release it into the All-That-Is! Let it become unified and merged. Freedom is merging. It is not severing the chains. It is not breaking the bonds, but it is to love the bondage and transmute it. Breaking is severance. It is an effort. Transmuting is allowance into divinity. That is what ascension is. *It is allowance into utter freedom through union with limitation.* Love and admire it for what it represents to you - a different facet of God I Am's creation. If you did not have boundaries and limitations, you would not have the differences between water, air and earth - and they are indeed magnificent. Freedom - that which is independence - is in dependence of all the aspects unto one another to create the whole. It is not severing. When you desire to transcend into an unlimited life, it is not leaving a lesser life behind. It is merging the lesser into wholeness, unlimitedness.

The jewel of life is captured within your heart. You do not see the reality that exists before you. You perceive reality as out there somewhere, far beyond your understanding called life on this plane. But *if you would appreciate life, you would experience reality.*

How many of you, when this evening is past, will capture the moon within your breast? How many of you saluted the sun this morn? It is real, is it not? It is part of your reality. How many of you said unto it: 'Divine being of light, I salute you! I resonate with joy and exhilaration for indeed you represent the reflection of reality that be I and you are a teacher and mirror and symbol of divine light! I salute you in the grandeur and magnificence that you are and in the knowing that I be also thus.' How many of you did this? This is your reality also, is it not? Did you even think of it? You are walking blindly, so desirous of being spiritual that you do not capture what is about you so that you may indeed go forth into unlimitedness. You are likened unto rats in a maze, but it is alright, there is no judgment here. I am merely giving you a perception that you have not considered before so that you may see the light, as it were, in a different aspect. There is no right and wrong. There is no better and best or good and bad. There only IS.

When you know of this and capture it within the cornucopia of your experience, you will then know God, and the glory of God will be exhibited within you. The second coming of Christ, or super-consciousness, will not occur until you embrace the wholeness as divine, including separation, limitation, bondage and suffering, whatever you judge it to be. It will not come. It will not be apparent unto you, until you know all of this as divine, as the creation of God I Am in a certain manifestation.

You are all your own slavemasters. You do it best when you do it unto yourself. You understand the idea of barrier and boundary as a containment device and not as a freeing device. It frees you to understand and appreciate what it is. Therefore, you have the freedom to soar around it once you know what it is, where it is, and understand its sovereignty. When you have had a barb in your rump you know its sovereignty. When you have had a head-on collision with a mountain, then you know its sovereignty. That is what the bird experiences when it first desires to exhibit its sovereignty over the mountains. Then it respects, allows, appreciates and then it soars in freedom, joyous and not fearful that it shall encounter this again. The river of life is golden if you will but see the gold within it and not the muck and the mire. It is not murky unless you perceive it this way and *perception is a choice.* Your barriers and your boundaries are choices. They are options. You focus on a certain reality and in that now moment all the other realities are, as you call it, on hold, and that is a choice. You place boundaries around a certain experience, but you may choose to understand the river of gold as flowing through you, rather than the mud, the muck, the mire and the murkiness.

There was an entity called Jean Pierre Ramon and he was a scientist. He published a paper, a scientific illustration of limited divine thought. The topic discussed the harmonics of sound, of the vibration called music. As he was a scientist he illustrated his endeavour through teaching in classrooms. However, through this paper, he became enamoured with music - he became a composer. He became enraptured with this beauty - it stirred his soul. Indeed, he became quite entranced with it until every moment was taken up with his discovery of harmonics. It spilled over into his classroom quite naturally and one of his students queried: 'Monsieur Ramon, how is it you compose? What is it that you do when you create such beauty, such splendour with tones?' And he said: 'I am freest to create beauty when I know my limitations.'

Do you know what this means? Do you understand it at all? When you understand what it is that you want to create, you have choices. You have options. It is called narrowing the options. As you create, you choose a particular note, a particular octave, a particular flow and you allow it to flow through you. Many times this choice is of soul level. It is not conscious and you channel your soul essence unto your paper. This is what he did. He understood the beauty and magnificence of the boundaries of the notes and the harmonics contained. Through this knowingness and the appreciation and embrace of it he created God. That is what art is. God exemplified.

You also can create beauteous symphonies of your life, string quartets, orchestrations and celestial choirs. They can all be your life if you will understand the beauty within the limitation. You may have the freedom to go through any octave you so desire, for when you recognize the limitation within an octave, that gives you the understanding of how to create beyond this limitation. You see, when you understand where the mountains are, you have the freedom to soar between them. Now, you will all go hence from here, I know this, and scratch your heads and say: 'What did all of that mean?' You will be frustrated with the limitations and boundaries in your life and you will gaze into the mirror and say: 'There is too much abundance of beauteous cell on this embodiment, and I am frustrated with this.' You will not embrace this limitation and so you will continue in separation, in disallowance, invalidating that which you judge. This is alright, but I wish you to know what it is that you do.

Your souls have cried out for eons to be unchained from your non-understanding of freedom. They have cried, and therefore the essence which be I has called upon the God of Gods and allowed its appearance in this manner, so that we may come unto you to illustrate freedom to you. 'I Am Free!!' you desire to say unto yourself, but what does this mean? What does it carry within it? How can you know freedom if you do not allow yourself the keys to freedom? The keys are love, light and laughter. Grand trinity. Trinity of divinity. Laughter is the buoyancy that will set you free when you otherwise would not be. Humour indeed is the juxtaposition of your life experiences against one another, so that it appears to be out of synch. Do you know what synch is? Synchronicity. Synchronicity is always apparent, even though it is not obvious. It is going beyond the obvious into the unobvious. That is what ascension is.

I so desire all of you to know freedom. Here it is. Take it if you want it. If you do not, there is no judgment, but do not go through life desiring a thing that you indeed may create if you so choose. I desire you to be free, to fly, to go forth into the unlimited dimension with that which be I. I do desire this. Freedom, unlimitedness, sovereignty, mutual admiration and respect of one God for another. That is freedom. I so want it for all of you. I want you all to be unfettered of judgment, of fear, of hatred.

I love you, beauteous Gods, all of you. Lights of the Universe, all! Go forth with this light and illuminate your pathway. Cast forth the flame of freedom within your breast and be the candle for others within the darkness. Allow them to experience admiration, respect and appreciation of that which they have previously judged to be limitation and lack of freedom. I love you and I want you to be free, but I cannot want for you what you do not want for yourself. Please remember, freedom is union with all, everything, every aspect, all of life. That is freedom. Then you may say to yourself and to the entire universe: 'I AM FREE. I AM FREE.' Remember love. That is freedom.

I am free. I will bid you all farewell for now. I love you.

Namaste.

Chapter 8

ST. GERMAIN'S STORY

The I AM Presence Of St. Germain
through Claire Heartsong.

Note: For the convenience of the audience assembled at this gathering, Allison Heartsong (Claire's soulmate) poses clarifying questions to St. Germain.

So it was that I did come to Terra, even as yourself, for I have loved so grandly this jewel in the heavens which you call your Mother Earth. I have loved this jewel of my breast and the process that you call ascension and the grand design of the Radiant One, the Father/Mother Source, who conceived all of this of which I am a part with you in its conception. We have been watching over her for a long time. We have been cuddling the wee ones, nudging and caressing and coming down to touch.

Indeed, the ascension is near and dear to my heart. The evolution of this planet, solar system and galaxy and the universe, indeed, all that has ever been conceived in the void of the Mother/Father God, I love with all my being. And so do you, that is why you are here. And alas, in the grand cycle of your time at the conclusion of what may be called another High-Renaissance, there is once again a desire for a grand enlightenment of the human mind and the establishment of a grander freedom.

So I invite you to relax, to be humoured and entertained and allow your doubts and your scepticism, for they too are wondrous and in due time the glass will clear and you will know your SELF.

133

So I encourage you to bring all of yourself here, every part of you, that I have more fully conversation with my SELF. You are my SELF and I am in profound awe and wonderment as I gaze upon the mirror of you to know more fully who I am. I honour your presence, the beauty that is arrayed before me. You are the jewels in my crown.

In that timing, long ago in your chronicles, when there was a burgeoning of humankind to know its Divinity, to be no longer controlled and enslaved quite so much, I came forth, once again to be a spark and I took upon me grand and wondrous dramas in the courts of Britain and Europe.

Indeed, my mother was queen of England[1] who epitomized the colonization of nations, which was part of her soul memory of 'star-wars'. Indeed beloveds, it is true - Queen Elizabeth was a grand fiery-haired one, to be sure, with a grand heart and a grand mind and a grand vision and a grand knowingness. She conceived that which be I and she sent me off onto other parentage, the home of the Bacons, where I became quite a boar[2].

A.H: So you are confirming that Francis Bacon[3] was the son of Queen Elizabeth who gave her son to one of the ladies in waiting[4].

Indeed.

And so he became Francis Bacon?

Quite a rowdy, to be sure and not altogether boring. I did gather to myself the ways and means of impressing others in the high places and a way of being quite witty and quite wondrous with verbiage. Yet do you know my beloveds, deep within my soul was a knowingness of who I be and of the design of my coming. The miracles occurred, appearances and 'encounters of the close kind'. Though I was yet a youngster, I was made aware as Francis Bacon of the knowingness of the ancients and where I had hidden certain treasures. I did find all of that, which was quite exciting - to open the box of myself, the time capsule, and to come into a completion in ascension in that lifetime.

---

1 Queen Elizabeth, (1533 - 1603) daughter of Henry VIII.
2 The boar was one of Francis Bacon's signature codes.
3 English Renaissance philosopher Francis Bacon (1561 - 1626).
4 A lady of rank who is a member of the royal household and in attendance on a queen or princess.

I staged the death (of Francis Bacon), that still has some scratching their heads, and continued on to work upon the European scene with a grand vision of union, a grand vision to be in the footsteps of that One who was my son, the One you call Jesus.

A.H: As I understand it, you are saying that even during your youth as Francis Bacon you became aware of soul memory, including your life as Joseph?

Indeed, not only soul memory, beloved, but that which I had buried in a variety of different places, actual tangible records that I had laid up for myself for a later time.

A.H: So in the middle of your life as Francis Bacon, you had awareness that you had these previous lifetimes and you had awareness of your mission, including the United States of America?

Indeed, what the planet was coming into, the shift from the Piscean understanding to the Aquarian and to the Era of God.

A.H:..that you were laying the foundation for that shift.

Yes, it burned brightly within me. I was entorched with the passion of it and so was that which was my mate, whose name was Portia.

A.H: And do I understand you to mean that at the end of the life of Francis Bacon an ascension or expansion of consciousness into seventh level occurred that did not involve physical death and reincarnating in a body, but simply staging a false death and burial so that you could continue as the embodiment of Francis Bacon now ascended as a seventh level ascended master and that you moved to Europe to continue as St. Germain?

Indeed.

A.H: Approximately how long was it from the time you staged the artificial death of Francis Bacon and moved from England to the European continent, before you met Portia?

We knew one another before.

A.H: Was she in a physical embodiment or in an etherical..?

In an embodiment. We knew - she knew better than I - we knew the purpose of the ascension was for Union.

A.H: You mean while you were living the life of Francis Bacon, you met Portia?

Yes. She too ascended in that timing. She lifted her frequency into a grand understanding of who she be, so that we might facilitate one another. Now, I did say unto you earlier, how it is that the identity of who we think ourselves to be can be quite tenacious. So it was with even that which be I. I was quite taken up with being an ascended master and my purpose.

A.H: You were also taken up with the identity of writing the King James version of the Bible.

That was all before, beloved. Yes, that is true. I was quite in awe of that which be I am.

A.H: And Portia suggested that there might be more?

Indeed. She was sort of a thorn in my side, allowing me to know. My beloved, do not get so caught up in this wondrous..

A.H: ..personification of the age of enlightenment?

That is a good way to put it. '..the enlightening of the human mind that you forget the greater part. This is but a step into that. It is but a part of the journey, so be you humble'. I thought I was surely the epitome of humility. She let me know that I was not.

A.H: You said: 'I am the personification of the age of enlightenment.' She said: 'There is more, you can be an ascended master'. You said: 'I am an ascended master' and she replied: 'There is more, it is called I AM union'.

Indeed. I thought: Is it not that we are to transcend all of this and enlighten ourselves and show humanity that what Jesus did they could do too? That the miracles he wrought, you could do too? That the grand alchemy of the embodiment, even the bringing forth of flawless jewels, is what you can do too, that you may drink the elixir of life and be renewed. Is that not enough? Surely, I thought. So I went around for two hundred years into the courts of Europe, exemplifying grand miracles. I was the wonder-man who never grew old[5].

---

5 Voltaire (real name Francois Marie Arouet, 1694 - 1778), french author and philosopher, reports having met and conversed with St. Germain at several occasions and describes his appearance as that of a man of forty-five years of age. When meeting St. Germain again forty years later, he expresses his puzzlement at St. Germain's unchanged appearance, still looking forty-five years of age.

A.H: For those who are not familiar with this fact, I wish to mention that there are historical records that St. Germain visited the courts of Europe (England, France, Germany, Russia, Austria, Italy) and people were amazed that after fifty or one hundred years he still looked the same age. He became known as the miracle man, the man who never died, between about 1620 and 1820.

So, it was not long after the ascension was made and St. Germain was donned as an identity, one of many I assumed, Portia was - the word would be mind-boggling to understand - but she took within her womb a conception to bear forth one who was in ripeness and readiness. Prior to the hour of delivery she had from time to time become quite, as it were, frustrated and upset with me for not choosing the grander part of visions that she was partaking in. I was not yet quite able to see her vision of I AM Union.

So she saw that in the grand scheme of things I was not allowing myself to partake of her heart's desire and knowing. And looking into the creation of another timing, she did see there would be a ripeness to fulfill her vision. So great was her love that she allowed me the realization of my vision. She was not in anger and not in frustration, when she dissipated the embodiment while in child birth. It was her love, her capacity to allow and to hold to the immaculate concept of yet another birth and another time, that released her from that particular drama to bring her forth into yet another incarnation, to shift the tragic to magic.

So, for two hundred years I was a vagabond and gypsy upon your plane and appeared quite miraculously without any dust upon my raiment and some exclaimed: 'But you were just in Paris yesterday and, my goodness, here you are in Brussels and there is not a speck of dust on you.' So I did pop in from time to time in wondrous ways to display much wisdom and my understanding of ascension.

There were many who entered mystery schools with me and became very enlightened, illumined beings.

And so, yes, I had a part to play with others in the founding of this country (U.S.A.). It was my intense desire to create a union of consciousness upon the land, a global community of enlightened beings in full realization of their power Source, no more to be enslaved and governed by any rule that would separate them. I did the best that I could in the uniting of the European nations into one Europe, but that went awry. I did what I could to inspire the founding fathers of this, your America, to be the land to receive the dove and the eagle into a merging of a union, to plant the seeds that a race of beings may come forth, an I AM race, America the Free. There is much love in my heart for this. Yet, do you know, my beloveds, when your Declaration of Independence was signed at a bit of coaxing from Uncle Sam (that be I) and your constitutional government was coming into an alignment and the factioning was lessening, I was still in my being very dissatisfied and I had a hunger and a thirst. I wondered, after all that had been realized at my hand and those that had the same vision that I had, why there was such an emptiness. Then I began to remember the invitation that had come to me two hundred years earlier.

A.H: I believe you gave a beautiful demonstration to this planet of what can be accomplished and what cannot be accomplished by an ascended master making an all-out effort to enlighten humanity.

Enlightenment can only be done from within. I chose the greater part and entorched myself so that the Brilliance of the God I AM might radiate and entorch every heart of humanity that I was not able to touch before as an individuated example. So I decided to come through the backdoor, so to speak.

A.H: To move from an individual approach to a universal approach?

Indeed. I would ask that while we are here that there be the allowing of a grand transmission of I AM flow, and there indeed has been that. Yet, should you want the More, even as I came to want the More with every cell of my being, then I invite you , too, to begin to ask. And I shall come unto you as your own I AM presence to stir you, to quicken you, to activate within your heart-seal the union.

When there began a swelling within every atom of the focus of my energies here upon your plane, an intensification beyond comprehension (you begin to get the feel of it, for this is the design of your being too, and of all of humanity eventually, to feel what I began to feel) I removed from my feet the shodding of fine leather fit to enter the throne rooms. I released from my shoulders the robes of ermine and velvet. Now it was time for me to enter into my passion upon the donkey of humility. It was time for me to come to know God I AM. It was time for me to release the grand design that I thought I had fulfilled - to be in honour of it, to be sure, but to allow the cup to be emptied.

So I walked and I went into the inner cities and I dipped my hands into the sup and ate of the brew of my brothers. I looked into the eyes of the prostitutes and I went into the prisons of spirit and body and I began to understand myself in a way that I had not done so previously. I began to see the twinkle in every eye, regardless of the tragedy, regardless of the drama, regardless of how they created the illusion that they were victims.

A.H: You began to feel the Christ in every heart.

And indeed, the Anti-Christus within my being, *the part within me* that crucified myself, *the part within me* that hung on the cross, the part within me that entered into the tomb, the part within me that rose again. I began to see that all - everyone around me was Christus, was God/Goddess. I began to behold the miracle in it all, in every grain of sand that my feet trod upon, in the lily, in the rose and in the thorn.

I became humbled and teachable; open and childlike and outrageous in my flamboyancy, my buoyancy, my capacity to bring smiles upon the faces of those who were downtrodden, to be the mirror. To allow the brownie camera of me to expand my focus by first allowing myself to be very small. Then I continued to expand and expand and expand my lens of perception of who I thought myself to be to begin to see through the lens of every point of view of you. At last I began to have an understanding of what I was after and that that was the power Source that fulfilled me, that sustained me. That empowerment was what brought ecstatic rapture unto my every cell rather than the emptiness that I had known as I aligned unto the altered-ego in order to come into merging - the ultimate freedom of empowered union.

A.H: *I would say you were consumed by the yearning for home.*

The yearning for Home, the yearning for AUM, the yearning for the true gold. Yea, I had been an alchemist - I thought I knew it all, but now I began to understand the true alchemy of God/man. When I placed my whole being upon the face of the Earth in grand supplication and yearning and released myself - in that hour, in that moment my beloved Portia was conceived, once again to take incarnation. For thirteen years I walked alone, yet I was not alone, for there was a knowingness, a new star was born. I knew something was 'up'.

Thirteen years later, wearing the garments of a labourer, my skin bronzed, my blue eyes a'twinkle, I entered into a wondrous vineyard. It was toward sunset - all was aglow and all the labourers had gone but one. I heard the lullaby of a lark and the warble of a tern that melted my heart. Through the verdant branches I saw before me the image of a young maiden. Classic in her profile, lithe of arm and leg, her hair silken, I was enraptured and in awe. I recognized her. She was caressing the grapes and singing unto each one a lullaby, their rich ruby lustre sparkling like gems within her hand. Such tenderness, such knowingness - such innocence.

I made myself known unto her and said: 'Come hither, young maiden,' and I did too avow from my throat, passages that even amazed me. I was so aquiver. A vibration began to overtake me that is not of this world. She said unto me, as I sung her praises: 'I am your mirror.' I had not heard this before. Now is this not a grand knowing from a thirteen-year old? She was a grand wise one indeed who knew what she was viewing and what she was feeling, and in her innocence she was teachable.

So it was as the sun began to emit its radiance of deepening violet hue and the diadems began to sprinkle themselves across the heavens, that we walked and held hands and allowed a flow, a presence to move within us, to move aside all else, to quicken every atom into all-knowingness. *Every* emotion, *every* experience of all humanity, all worlds, all creation poured into us as tidal waves and we held to one another. We became a conduit. We began to understand the true meaning of masculine-feminine, the electromagnetic energy flow. The Divine Mother of all embraced us and held us in the cup of her heart, else we could not have withstood the experience - it was so intense.

There was not even the whisper of a thought of what could be called a sexual nature that flit across my mind. There was intense circulation, intercourse beyond imagining that occurred with us. All soul memory of the All-That-Is came into our consciousness and our consciousness merged into every atom. As the sun arose we merged in the light of the Radiant One. *That* my beloved is my body. *You* are my body. *This* is my body [pointing to the channel's body and touching a nearby rose], *this* is my body [indicating the audience and all within and beyond the room]. *This* is the Allness that the wondrous teachers of all ages taught, even that which be I in past incarnations. *That* is the home to which we yearn to return. It is an expansion beyond that which the Father/Mother birthed before we came into form. *That* Body is Home, the Radiant One, the Christus that is coming to be birthed through you, a new All That Is that you are now merging with. This grand light[6] that is moving through your heavens ever closer in the illusion of time/space, is raising your frequency. The vibration that you are feeling now is moving you closer to the AUM stretch, the Source, the Golden Brilliance of the God I AM that this light is but a reflection of.

Every step of it, the involution and the evolution, the implosion and the explosion, every choice of creation is divinely embraced into this Radiant One that I AM. I come as a witness of this ascension - *the ultimate ascension to be God I AM*. You are star-seeded for this.

So, allow this to be a spark of re-co-gnition. I love you - I AM you. You are the Radiant One that I AM. In this timing you are the hands and feet who carry the I AM Presence upon the land. In flamboyant

---

6 Reference pertains to the photon belt.

humility be in appreciation of *all* experience that comes unto you, for it *is* you. Allow that Divine Maternal energy which once dissipated its focus to have full embodiment in you, that you may *be* the Divine Mother. Only in this way may the warrior be released of its bondage of illusion that there are two rather than One and that those two are at war with one another.

I bring you tidings of the God I AM, of the Christus within you, the All-Knower within yourself. I would ask before we depart that you allow a moment or two of silence wherein you may all bask and where this One may enter in if you choose, to feel, to lay aside and to allow an expansion. You are laying aside your veils and you are entering a new life. Until we meet again, know that ascension is your destiny and you are realizing it in every now.

Namaste, my dear ones.

Chapter 9

PORTIA'S STORY.

The I AM Presence Of Portia
(St. Germain's Twin Soul)
Through Claire Heartsong.

As I feel your hearts and your wanting in this hour of communion together, do understand more fully who it is who forever embraces you, cradles you and wipes your wee tears. I come forth to breathe upon you in the silence, in the tenderness of this moment, in the form of a story; not that you shall become attached to the story, or that you allow it to become dogma, or that you perceive me as special, or that this was something that occurred long ago and does not have relevancy now - but in listening to the vibrations beyond the words I desire to stroke you through that which pours forth through these lips to nurture you, to caress you, so that you can remember how it used to be in that for which you have longed and to assist you to know that it is always here. It is within you - it is without you. You are coming more and more into this embrace all the time and I desire to assist you through this story, so that you will not be quite so afraid of losing yourself in this embrace. Indeed, you shall be more of who you really are, for I shall pour myself into you. So I invite you, my dear hearts, and I shall cradle you in these moments that we are together.

Long ago, in what you term time, about four hundred years ago and plus, the story is set in the merry land of the Angles/Angels[1].

From the etheric realms I looked down through the dimensions into that which is the Earth, during a time of great awakening, a time

---

1 England

when the land that had previously been very asleep and darkened, was now awakening into a grand, grand dawning.

Ones who previously had laid seed for this hour were taking embodiment again to set forth into motion a movement and a flow that would affect the entire course of events in history for the centuries to come. It would pave the way for a new race - an I AM race.

As I looked down from my place beyond this dimension I did behold a magnificent lot of beings who preceded me and one of whom was as myself, in male embodiment. I watched him and watched over him upon the birthing bed when he was delivered in great secrecy and great shrouding. There were hushed whispers and dimmed lights when the cries of birthing broke forth through the dry lips of the mother with her flaming red hair. My heart ached for her and for the sibling who was born. The young maiden, who was a lady in waiting, took the wee babe before he even had a suckle at the breast of the mother. She bore him away to a relatively modest cottage, by comparison to the room in which this babe was born. She had given forth a still-born and her breasts ached with the milk that fed this babe.

Years passed and I continued to look down, longing to romp and to play with this one. He saw me with inner vision and he wished to draw me into his experience, but I said it was not time yet. Other ones, such as myself in the ethers, participated and from time to time manifested and taught this wee lad and opened him far beyond his years or beyond the capacity of those around him who were indeed great beings. This one had a work to do and it was agreed by the councils that a great focus would come through him to be embodied and exemplified, that would entorch the entire court of England with a new thought, a new capacity to perceive life.

He was a lad when he took a number of grand pilgrimages. He followed the steps of a previous embodiment that he had known as Merlin[2] - one of the Merlins. There was with him in the court one who previously had walked with him as Arthur[3]. There were others as

---

2 Magician and seer, helper of King Arthur.
3 Reference is to Arthur, King of Britain and hero of the Round Table; supposed to have lived in the sixth century A.D.

well who took re-embodiment to gather again at the great Round Table[4] of consciousness that would draw down the heavens into Earth and lift up the humanity that had been so asleep for so long since the timing of that great One who sealed his life into the tomb and then arose.

So, the years passed and the grandeur that was England captured the minds and the adventuresome spirit of an awakening race. Ships set sail and conquered distant lands and marriages were taking place to wed the courts of many nations and to begin a union which was so heartfelt by this one whom I loved.

In the laboratories this one secreted himself away with a few others who had a knowingness or a remembering of the roles that they had played in previous eras upon the land. In these secret places there were scores and scores and scores of books. There were vessels that contained elements, herbs and metals of many kinds. For hours and days these ones would secret themselves away and look upon the ancient tablets which had survived and which had been carried by a Brotherhood through the ages, for it was time to bring forth a grand alchemy; not just to produce gold to be worn upon the body, to bejewel the tables and the high ones in their courts, but to bring forth an understanding of the gold within the human soul, to transfigure and transmute the body, to bring forth the elixir of everlasting life and to bring forth a teaching and an awareness that would go forth upon the land and exemplify unto all who had ears to hear, how they might do this for themselves so they may be free.

So it was that this one, with a number of other ones, was privy to many, many books and records of bygone eras and they went on pilgrimages together. They went to what had become known as Alexandria and other temple sites in Egypt, the Holy Land, Asia Minor, Greece, Italy, Germany, Austria and Switzerland, where some of these records were hidden away by the Habsburgers in their courts. They were vagabonds sealed to one another in fellowship by orders

---

4 The large circular table at which King Arthur and his knights used to sit, giving its name to an order of knighthood instituted by the King.

which they honoured and perpetuated.

As this one [St. Germain] was drawing close to a knowing that it was time to say adieu, (he had rendered quite a wondrous Elizabethan drama and had stewed and embroiled himself quite grandly in intrigue and the judiciaries were, shall we say, on his neck a good bit of the time), he desired to withdraw and to participate with humanity in more of a quiet manner and to come forth in a more empowered manner with a grand design that was beginning to hatch within his heart.

So it was that as he began to withdraw himself that I did make my appearance. I will not go so much into that story of that particular rendezvous - it was glorious - and we did come together. Both of us came into an understanding of what is called the breath of life and raised ourselves into what is termed the ascension. We both staged quite a wondrous release of our embodiments and for some, that was quite a relief, and for others there was a knowing that all was well, they knew the design.

Perhaps at another timing, this one - that is my mate, the beloved St. Germain - can share with you more fully that story from his perspective, as indeed he already has. For myself, there was a growing understanding not ever forgotten. I had an encounter in the ethers with my beloved brother Yeshua, my beloved sister Mary Magdalena, my sister and mother Isis and my brother and father Osiris and other beings who knew that the cycles of the Earth were coming into a consummation at the birthing of the Aquarian Age. I knew I had a part to play in this, so I chose to delay my coming until the appropriate hour and then there was the descent into an embodiment here.

Together with my beloved, I did enter into a great adventure, an adventure called union with the All-That-Is. To assist in that union there was an entity who desired to come forth to participate in the trinity to assist us into the embrace into one instant of all energy flows that have ever been and will yet be. This entity came forth into my womb and all was prepared. It became increasingly apparent that my beloved, while he too desired Union, was not yet ready for that for which I had come. Therefore the babe and myself, in childbirth, took our exit to allow my beloved an opportunity to come into a ripeness and to do that which was his dream, which was to bring forth a union of nations and peoples and a raising of consciousness. His dream was a liberation of the minds that had been darkened for so long, to assist them to know who they be, to follow in the footsteps of Yeshua and show unto these ones that all that this one did, they could do as well.

So he went on his way. For two hundred years he traversed the lands of Europe. As an ascended master he was not limited to that arena. He sowed seeds in that timing which are now germinating and bearing fruit over this entire planet. It became clear that every effort he was making was being frustrated, even though there was wondrous evolvement and enlightenment. My hunger and knowing gradually became his hunger and his intense yearning to realize.

After the seeding of the United States and her independence from the mother-land, my beloved began to grow troubled within his breast - yes, this is possible for an ascended master. He began to feel the agony for the sickness that was so rampant upon the land, the separation, the warring, the diseasement and the disempowerment. When the night was darkest for his soul, I appeared to him. We had of course congress before with one another, but our hearts' deepest desire could only be accomplished with us both being in physical embodiment.

So I made appearance unto him and we made an agreement. In that instant my energies were stepped down and I was conceived. I chose to be born as all humanity is, to be humble, to be as a child, to embrace all humanity into my heart - to be no different than you, my brothers and my sisters. I retained enough of the knowing and had about me angels and beings who assisted me to remember who I am and why I had come into the Earth-plane again.

One grand day, just beyond my twelfth birthday, I was in my father's vineyard. In this season, already a bit of frost had settled and the leaves of the grapes had begun to turn. The grapes were full and fragrant and heavy with the ruby. The sun was drifting downward, the labourers had gone to their homes and I delayed my returning to the hearth. The birdsong was so sweet and invited me into a trill and a lullaby as I walked in the midst of the vineyard, cradled the grapes in my hands and sampled their sweetness. The glory of the sunset was so magnificent on that night and the rising evening star a diamond, close enough that I could touch and place it on my heart.

In that instant, as I reached out to the star, I chanced to look just across the way and beheld the form of a man. I realized he had been there for some time and I understood he was not one of the labourers, but I did recognize that this indeed was my beloved. He did bring himself forth unto me and did extol my virtues. I said unto him: 'My dear brother, I am your mirror.' Hand-in-hand we walked that night and we merged the energies of all time and all space.

He did not take advantage of my virginity, for that was not even whispered across our thoughts, but we did merge with one another that night. As the sun began to rise, so did we begin to be lifted by the arms of the Father/Mother, our Source and we did melt into the Sun/ Son of our being. We did birth ourselves anew into the Union that forever is. We did birth ourselves into every atom, into every dimension, into every thought and into every feeling that is the God I AM.

I share with you this story, so that you too may be the Mirror unto your brothers and sisters, and be as the Rose within the garden of God. Honour yourselves, love yourselves, deliver yourselves into the majesty, into the frequency of the forevermore that I AM. I love you. I AM You.

Namaste.

MESSAGE FROM THE STARS

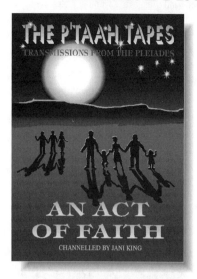

THE P'TAAH TAPES

TRANSMISSIONS FROM THE PLEIADES

CHANNELLED BY JANI KING

Both books: Size A5, 260 pages, soft cover cello-glazed.

Something very unusual and very special took place in the latter half of the year 1991. Amidst the tropical setting of the coastal hills of North Queensland, Australia, a group of people gathered regularly for twenty-eight weeks to listen to the teachings of one of the star-people: P'taah from the constellation of the Pleiades.

At a time of a humanity stressed to the hilt and suffering as never before from the effects of a fear-based consciousness, the denial of the God within, P'taah's communication could not have been timed more appropiately. P'taah prepares humanity for the forthcoming transition from separation to Oneness. If there ever was a message of limitless love, of joy and upliftment, of concrete thought applicable to practical, every day living, then it is this material; though much of it shakes the bedrock of belief structures which constitute human reality.

P'taah tells of the grand changes to come for humanity and the planet Earth. He opens our vista to a universe teeming with life. He speaks of the inner Earth people and the star-people and in doing so, assures us that we are not alone. What is more, he presents us with the panacea to transmute fear into love, to discover who we really are. Gently he dissolves the imprisoning shackles of dogma and concept, which lock Man into a consciousness of survival thinking, and reveals, contrary to all appearances, an irresistible, breathtakingly beautiful destiny for Mankind.

The love of the star-people for humanity could not be expressed any better than in P'taah's own words:

WE WILL DO ANYTHING TO BRING YOU HOME!

TRIAD®

From Tragic To Magic

In January 1991, in the tropical North of Queensland, Australia, several energies from the unseen and one of the star-people, P'taah from the constellation of the Pleiades, began to implement a plan to help humanity through the final stages of the great transition. The book 'GOD I AM - From Tragic To Magic', inspired by the Triad of Isis, Immanuel and St. Germain, is the first in a series of publications born of this undertaking.

GOD I AM

From Tragic To Magic

Peter O. Erbe

*Size A5, 250 pages,
soft cover cello-glazed.*

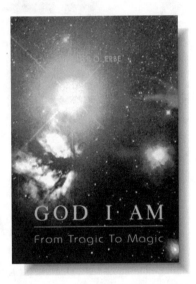

Every 25,000 years our Solar System completes one orbit around Alcione, the central sun of the Pleiades, a constellation at a distance of approximately 400 light years from our Sun. In 1961 science discovered a photon belt which encircles the Pleiades at a right angle to its orbital planes. Our Sun, and Earth with it, is entering this Photon belt between now and the year 2011.

The photon belt is the cosmic 'trigger force' to shift humanity from third level into fourth level density, from separation into Oneness. Thus, the magnitude and beauty of this event Earth is preparing for defies any description. Earth and humanity are aligning for its birth into Christ-consciousness - the union of Star Light with matter - the marriage of Spirit with separated Selves.

As the night transforms into a new day, so is the Age of Darkness giving way to the Age of Light. It is the greatest event ever to grace the Earth and her children. Terms such as New Age, Super-consciousness, etc., are but different labels for one and the same occurrence. It is the 'end-time' of the prophecies, for time as such shall cease to be. Ageing, ailments and sorrow shall be no more. To partake of this grandest of events, man must be aligned with its energy.

Humanity, as such, is governed by false perception, the adherence to the frequency of fear, the result of which is literally an upside down perception of life. Only that which is aligned with Light can partake of Light, thus those not aligned with the cosmic current of energy flow - the Divine Intent - shall sleep the long sleep.

It is the purpose of this material to develop the magnificent tool of True Perception with which we align for the birth into the dawn of a new day in creation, the Age of Love. As the chrysalis is the bridge between caterpillar and the butterfly, so is True Perception the bridge between third level and fourth level density, between separation and Oneness.

The universe with all its beings, in seen and unseen dimensions, joins with us in the grandest of all celebrations, the jubilance of rebirth into Light - the dance of the Gods - for where Earth, and we as her children go, is the fulfilment of the soul's ancient cry:

WE ARE COMING HOME

TRIAD®

FROM THE COUNCIL OF LIGHT COMES:

ST.GERMAIN
EARTH'S
BIRTH
CHANGES

ST. GERMAIN
THROUGH AZENA

ISBN: 0 646 21388 1

*Size A5, 280 pages
soft cover, cello-glazed*

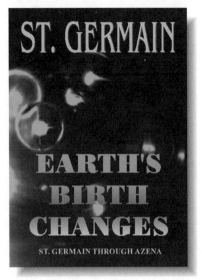

The upheavals, the unrest and torment within humanity at this time are the contractions and labour pains heralding a birth of an incomprehensible, cosmic magnitude. The decade before and after the turn of the century represent the culmination - the Harmonic Convergence - of a 200 million year evolutionary cycle: Earth and her children, in unison with the Solar system and thousands of galaxies, are birthing into a new dimension.

From the shores of eternal being, from the Council of Light, comes one called St. Germain to assist in this birthing process. As he bares his heart in love and compassion, rekindling an ancient memory, he transforms the prophecies of Old, of looming calamities and trepidation, into shining, new horizons without circumference. His words are carried by an air of urgency for the changes are imminent; quote: 'the acceleration is becoming exponential'. His gift to us is not approximate statement but the promise of fact: freedom for humanity.

Casting a light across the past 20 million years of Earth's history and evolution, he reveals fascinating facts about our origin, about the star-seeding of humanity, about our forefathers from the Pleiades, the Orion constellation, Lyra and more. The startling details of the rise and demise of ancient Lemuria and Atlantis leave us in suspense.

What is more, he unfolds a vision for humanity of such grandeur, that it renders the uninitiated speechless. If the historian and the scientist only as much as consider the information presented here, they will have to revise their certainties, for their facts are at risk. Unravelling a tapestry of dazzling beauty for humanity, the thrilling joy of St. Germain's message is contagious, is of effervescence and jubilance: the transition from separation to the union of Oneness with all Life - the age of Love -

THE GOLDEN OF GOD

TRIAD®